THE BIBLE IN POLITICS

THE BIBLE
IN POLITICS

How to Read the Bible Politically

Richard Bauckham

Westminster/John Knox Press
Louisville, Kentucky

First published in Great Britain 1989
SPCK, Holy Trinity Church, Marylebone Road
London NW1 4DU

Copyright © Richard Bauckham 1989

First American edition

Published by Westminster/John Knox Press
Louisville, Kentucky

PRINTED IN THE UNITED STATES OF AMERICA
9 8 7 6 5 4 3 2 1

Library of Congress Cataloging-in-Publication Data

Bauckham, Richard.
    The Bible in politics : how to read the Bible politically /
Richard Bauckham. — 1st American ed.
        p.   cm.
    Includes index.
    ISBN 0-664-25088-2

    1. Christianity and politics—Biblical teaching.
2. Sociology, Biblical. 3. Bible—Hermeneutics.
4. Bible—Criticism, interpretation, etc.   I. Title.
BS680.P45B38 1989
220.8'32—dc20   89-34903
                                                                    CIP

*To friends in
South Africa and Namibia,
with gratitude for a
memorable visit in 1987.*

Contents

Preface

This book had its beginnings in a series of seven articles published in 1984—5 in *Third Way* magazine, which has done much in recent years to promote Christian political awareness in Britain. I am grateful to the editor Tim Dean for inviting me to write the articles and also for inviting me and encouraging me to expand them into a book. Without his initiative the book would not have been written.

Special thanks are also due to Philip Alexander, Arnold Anderson, Jonathan Chaplin and John Goldingay, who read all or parts of the book and made valuable comments.

It would be quite impossible to thank all who, over many years, have helped to form my thinking about biblical interpretation and biblical politics. The footnotes tend to record only more recent debts, and I am well aware that insights which seem to me original probably derive from sources I tapped long ago and have forgotten. Similarly, I need not say, in the usual fashion, that the faults are all mine, only that I cannot remember their sources! But hermeneutics, after all, is not an individual activity, but a corporate, co-operative task of the whole Church of Christ. The greater my debts to others, the more chance I have of helping my readers to contribute to that ongoing task.

Richard Bauckham
Handforth, May 1988

Acknowledgements

We are grateful to the following for permission to use copyright material:

Ravan Press Ltd, Johannesburg, for the extract from the poem 'Come, Freedom Come' by Walter M. B. Nhlapo.

World Council of Churches Publications for the psalms by Zephania Kameeta.

Chapter 9 is adapted from an article which first appeared in *Churchman*.

Scripture quotations from the Revised Standard Version of the Bible, copyrighted 1946, 1952, c 1971, 1973 by the Division of Christian Education of the National Council of the Churches of Christ in the USA, are used by permission.

THE BIBLE IN POLITICS

Introduction

Many Christians have recently been rediscovering the political dimension of the message of the Bible. This is really a return to normality, since the notion that biblical Christianity has nothing to do with politics is little more than a modern Western Christian aberration, which would not have been entertained by the Church in most periods and places of its history. But political interpretation of the Bible has many pitfalls for the unwary. It is all too easy to read our own prejudices into the Bible, while it is not at all easy to move intelligently, without anachronism, between the political societies of biblical times and the very different societies of today. The aim of this book is to help the reader towards an understanding of the political relevance of the Bible which will be both more disciplined and more imaginative than some current attempts to read the Bible politically. It offers neither a summary of the political teaching of the Bible nor a programme for Christian political action, but a prerequisite for those things: a course in political hermeneutics. In other words—lest the word *hermeneutics* put some people off—it is for those who want to know *how* to interpret the Bible politically. Along the way we shall reach many particular conclusions about the teaching of the Bible and its relevance to modern political issues, but these are essentially illustrations of a method which readers are encouraged to pursue for themselves. Although they cover quite a lot of biblical and political ground, they are a representative sample, not an exhaustive survey.

The first chapter is methodological: an introduction to hermeneutical issues and principles which will then be illustrated in practice in the rest of the book. Biblical interpretation is more of an art than an exact science. Like all art it has its rules and requires considerable discipline, but good interpretation is much more than a matter of following rules which can be learned in advance. Hence, after the first chapter, this book aims to teach by involving the reader in the practice of hermeneutics. Five chapters (2—6) offer examples of the political exegesis of specific, relatively short biblical passages. These sample texts have been selected for their diversity: they represent different types of biblical literature and relate to a fairly broad range of political issues. And, since the hermeneutical approach pursued in these chapters is to interpret the texts not in isolation but in relation to the rest of Scripture, they often range further than the passages to which they are anchored. The focus, however, in these chapters is on the detailed exegesis of particular texts, without which any biblical interpretation is bound to be shoddy and insecure.

A different, equally necessary approach to the biblical material is illustrated by chapter 7, in which a particular theme is traced through the whole Bible and the broad contours of its treatment in the Bible are delineated and developed. Chapters 8 and 9 bring parts of the Bible which few readers would expect to have modern political relevance into relationship with two of the most characteristically modern of political facts. The aim is to show how a creative encounter between the biblical texts and the modern realities can generate fresh insight, and so how the Bible can prove itself relevant in quite novel as well as well-tried ways. For it to do so is quite essential if a political hermeneutic is to be at all adequate to the needs of political praxis in the contemporary world. Finally, a concluding reflection steps beyond exegesis into theological and political reflection on the unifying centre of Scripture: Jesus and his salvific activity.

There is no reason why this book should be read in order. Not even the first chapter need be read first by those who prefer to reflect on methodology only after observing it in action. The other chapters may be read in whatever order a reader's interests suggest. My only request is that readers try not to prejudge the political relevance of the various parts of the Bible. Open-minded readers of Scripture will always have challenging and stimulating surprises in store for them.

To keep the function of this book in perspective, it may be worth recalling a remark made by Charles Williams about understanding the book of Job. He pointed out that there are many commentaries and exegetical studies available, and in their absence even the book of Job itself could be consulted.[1] I hope that the following chapters will lead readers not away from the biblical text, but constantly back to it, and into closer engagement with it.

1: Issues in Interpretation

In this chapter we shall discuss some of the most important hermeneutical issues that arise in applying the Bible to politics and formulate some principles for reading the Bible politically, before illustrating these principles in detailed examples of exegesis in subsequent chapters. We begin with one of the most crucial hermeneutical issues, which accounts for many differences between Christians on political matters: the relation between the Old and New Testaments.

Varieties of Biblical Politics
Most readers of the Bible notice an obvious difference between the Old Testament and the New Testament in their treatment of political matters. On a superficial view, at least, the Old Testament seems to have much to say about politics, the New Testament rather little. However, this may be a misleading way of stating the difference, since it ignores the extent to which New Testament material which is not very explicitly political may nevertheless have political implications. It is not so easy to be non-political as some people think. The difference between the testaments might be better expressed in terms of a difference of political context. Much of the Old Testament is addressed to a people of God which was a political entity and for much of its history had at least some degree of political autonomy. The Old Testament is therefore directly concerned with the ordering of Israel's political life, the conduct of political affairs, the formulation of policies, the responsibilities of rulers as well as subjects, and so on. The New Testament is addressed to a politically powerless minority in the Roman Empire. Its overtly political material therefore largely concerns the responsibilities of citizens and subjects who, though they might occasionally hope to impress the governing authorities by prophetic witness (Matt. 10.18), had no ordinary means of political influence. Their only conceivable (though scarcely practical) route to political power would have been that of armed revolt, an option which they seem to have rejected.

This difference between the testaments explains why, from the time of Constantine onwards, whenever the political situation of Christians has moved towards more direct political influence and responsibility, the Old Testament has tended to play a larger part in Christian political thinking than the New Testament. This has been the case not only in the classic 'Christendom' situation of much of Western Christian history, where the confessedly Christian society bore an obvious resemblance to political Israel. It can also quite often be seen in situations where Christians have supported revolutionary movements and in modern pluralistic democracies. In the course of Christian history Old Testament law and precedent have been used to support an extraordinary variety of political institutions and policies: such as divine-right monarchy, crusades, redistribution of wealth, use of the death penalty, aid for the Third World, and royal authority over national churches. The Old Testament has been used to argue both the admissibility and the inadmissibility of female rulers, slavery and political assassination.

The Problem of Selectivity

One of the problems which the history of Christian political use of the Old Testament highlights is that of selectivity. Clearly Christians have always *selected* those elements of Old Testament teaching which they consider to have contemporary political relevance, and in different times and places they have selected different elements. The problem here is that this selection has all too often been governed by expedience rather than by any hermeneutical principle, and it has therefore been in danger of being an ideological manipulation of Scripture to support current principles and programmes. It can be very salutary for modern Christians to compare their own selective use of Old Testament material with that of their predecessors, and to ask whether they have any principles which justify the one over against the other. How many of those who freely quote the prophets' demands for social justice in favour of the poor and oppressed, while ignoring, for example, the prophets' demand, sometimes in the same breath (Ezek. 22.7−8; Amos 8.4−6), for sabbath observance, do so in the light of a hermeneutical *principle*? For nineteenth-century sabbatarians, support for legislation to enforce national sabbath observance had the same significance−in being a crucial issue of

Christian obedience in the political sphere—as concern for the unemployed or the Third World has for many Christians today. In Old Testament terms, at least, they had a point.

Dispensational Differences

When Christians are asked to explain why an Old Testament political provision should not, in their view, be applied to present-day political circumstances, they most often make one of two types of response. One is an appeal to a difference of cultural context: what made political sense in ancient Israelite society may not do so in modern technological society. This is a consideration which applies equally to the relevance of New Testament teaching and will be discussed later in the chapter. Alternatively, however, appeal may be made to a difference of 'dispensational' context: in other words, to the pre-Christian character of the Old Testament. It is here that the relation between the two testaments becomes a vital issue. In fact, this appeal can itself take two rather different forms:

1. It can be argued that New Testament ethics, say in the Sermon on the Mount, are an advance on Old Testament ethical teaching, which therefore becomes to some extent obsolete.
2. It can be argued that Old Testament Israel was in the unique position of being a theocratic state, and cannot therefore provide a political model for the New Testament era, in which God's people are not a political entity but scattered throughout the nations. (In passing, it may be noted that in fact the Old Testament itself faced the political issues of a diaspora people of God, and provided not only some guidance for Jewish subjects of pagan states (Jer. 29), but also examples of Jews exercising political authority or influence in pagan states: Joseph, Daniel and his friends, and Esther and Mordecai.)

Both these forms of argument are used, for example, to render Old Testament wars inapplicable as political precedents. On the basis of the first argument, Old Testament teaching on war is often said to be replaced by Jesus' ethic of non-violence. On the basis of the second, Israel's wars were holy wars, waged by God against his enemies, but modern states cannot claim such divine sanction for their wars.

We need to be clear that, though they both depend on the dispensational position of the Old Testament, these are two quite different arguments. Both may have their place in a consideration of the biblical teaching on war. It is also worth noticing that both arguments involve us in another issue which we shall shortly take up: the relation between the people of God and the world. In the case of the first, if the argument is valid, we still need to know whether Jesus' ethic prohibits war only for Christian believers, or for secular states also. In the case of the second, we need to consider how far it is true that God governed his own people Israel on principles quite different from those he expects of other nations. Clearly the question of the modern relevance of Old Testament political material is a complex hermeneutical issue.

Using the Old Testament Today

In view of this complexity, some may be tempted to dismiss the political relevance of the Old Testament altogether. But there is a good reason for not doing so. God and his purposes for human life remain the same in both testaments, and it is primarily the character of God and his purposes for human life which are expressed in the political material of the Old Testament. They are expressed in forms appropriate to the specific conditions of Old Testament Israel: both the specific cultural context (or contexts) of a nation living in that time and place, and also the specific salvation-historical context of the national people of God in the period before the coming of Christ. This means that, while the law and the prophets cannot be *instructions* for our political life, they can be *instructive* for our political life. We cannot apply their teaching directly to ourselves, but from the way in which God expressed his character and purposes in the political life of Israel we may learn something of how they should be expressed in political life today.

This means that our first concern should not be to select those parts of the Old Testament which still apply today. None of it applies directly to us, as *instructions*, but all of it is relevant to us, as *instructive* (cf. 2 Tim. 3.16). Various aspects of Old Testament politics will prove instructive in different ways, as we consider both the differences and the similarities between their context, both cultural and salvation-historical, and ours. Not only analogous but also contrasting situations can be instructive. In every case we shall have to consider the salvation-historical context and relate the Old Testament material to the New Testament. The fundamental point about the relation between the testaments is not that in some

6

cases Old Testament provisions are superseded by the New Testament, while in other cases they are left unchanged. The fundamental point is that Jesus *fulfilled* the whole of the law and the prophets. None of the Old Testament can be unaffected by its fulfilment in Christ, but all of it, as fulfilled in Christ, remains instructive. We should not force this fulfilment in Christ into some artificial scheme (such as the traditional claim that Christ abrogated the civil and ceremonial law, but left the moral law in force), but should consider each part and aspect of the Old Testament in the light of Christ. The effect of doing this will take a wide variety of forms. We should also not forget that, just as we read the Old Testament in the light of its fulfilment in the New, so we must also read the New Testament against the background of the Old Testament, which it presupposes. In their political teaching, as in other matters, the two testaments supplement and inform each other.

Personal and Political Ethics

In addition to the question of the relation between the testaments, there are at least three other hermeneutical issues which constantly arise in considering the Bible's relevance to politics. These all affect our judgement about the extent of the biblical material that is relevant to modern politics. Has this or that passage something to say to our political life? 'No, because it is about personal ethics, not politics,' we sometimes say. Or: 'No, because it is about the social life of the Church, and cannot be applied to society outside the Church.' Or: 'No, because it applied to the particular cultural conditions of that time and cannot apply to our very different kind of society.' We need to look rather closely at these three sets of distinctions before we can decide what is and what is not politically relevant.

We begin with a hermeneutical principle which can be and has been used to render much biblical—especially New Testament—teaching irrelevant to political issues: the principle of a radical distinction between the ethical principles which apply to immediate personal relations and those which apply to political institutions and activities. According to this principle, the Sermon on the Mount would apply to a politician in her private life, but not in her public activity *qua* politician. An influential form of this view, though not its most extreme form, was held by Martin Luther. He pointed out, for example, that a judge who in his private life is obliged to forgive personal injuries against himself and not to demand reparation is equally obliged in his public capacity as a judge to pass sentence on criminals and not to let them off without punishment.

Luther did not make the mistake of arguing that *wholly* different ethical principles apply in the private and the public spheres. He did not, for example, distinguish love as the principle of personal ethics from justice as the ethical principle of public life—a distinction not to be found in the Bible. On the contrary, Luther recognized that the command to love one's neighbour (on which, according to Matt. 22.40, the *political* requirements of the law and prophets depend) was the ethical principle of government as well as of private life. But love must take different forms in public and private life.

To some extent he had a valid point. When Jesus' ethical teaching becomes specific it is most often with reference to personal life. Matthew 5.38—42, for example, is not addressed to judges as judges, but to private individuals. But it is doubtful whether any sharp distinction can be drawn between public and private life in the way that Luther's principle seems to require. The individual is obliged to forgive personal injuries against himself, but this principle will not be enough to guide him in situations where the interests of several people are involved, where other people have been injured or need protection, or where (as a parent, for example) he has a responsibility for the moral education of the person who has done wrong. In such situations forgiveness becomes one duty of love among others. But then no radical difference occurs when we move into political situations. The principle of forgiveness does not become inapplicable, but needs to take appropriate forms in conjunction with other principles of love.

Thus we have the ordinary Christian ethical task of applying the principles of Jesus' teaching to all the varying situations of life, including the political ones. Of course they will not all apply in all situations (Matt. 5.27—8 will have little relevance to, say, the problem of the arms race), but they must simply be allowed to apply where they do apply. There should be no hermeneutical rule which excludes them from the political sphere.

Ethics for the Church and for the World
Another way of limiting the application of New Testament ethics can also be illustrated from the sixteenth century. Whereas Luther

drew a sharp distinction between the private and the public roles of the Christian, the Anabaptists drew a sharp distinction between Christians and others, the Church and the world. The ethics of the Sermon on the Mount, they claimed, govern the whole life of the Christian community but are irreconcilable with the tasks of governing a state, so Christians may not hold public office in the state. Political activity must be left to non-Christians, to whom the Sermon on the Mount is not addressed and of whom a different ethical standard is required. It should be noticed that the extent to which all citizens are implicated in the activities of government, for example by paying taxes, raised problems for this view even in the sixteenth century. In modern democracies the difficulties are greater.

It is one thing to say that Christians should have both the motivation and the spiritual resources to live better lives than others (cf. Matt. 5.46−8) and to realize the intentions of God for human community more perfectly in the Church than elsewhere. It is another thing to say that differing ethical principles apply to Christians and to others. It is hard to find biblical support for the latter.

This being so, it not only follows that the Sermon on the Mount requires political as well as other forms of implementation. It also follows that fundamental New Testament principles for life in the Christian community extend in principle to life in human community as such, and therefore have political relevance. This applies, for example, to Jesus' revolutionary principle of authority as service (Mark 10.42−5), Paul's principle of sexual and racial equality (Gal. 3.28), his effective abolition of the status of slave (Philem. 16), and his principle of equality of material possessions (2 Cor. 8.14). It is to the great credit of the early Anabaptists that they took some of these principles more seriously in their primary application to the Christian community than their Protestant contemporaries did, and they were able to do this because they maintained a clear distinction between the Church and the world. But such principles, once recognized, cannot be confined to the Church. This was seen, for example, by the nineteenth-century Evangelicals who worked to abolish slavery not only as a status within the Church but also as a condition sanctioned by the state. It is seen by South African Christians who realize that if apartheid is unjustifiable in the Church it is unjustifiable in the state and society too.

In extending New Testament principles of Christian community beyond the Church to political society we must take full account of the differences. Politics cannot do what the gospel and the Spirit can do, and politics cannot do in all societies what it can do in a society deeply influenced by Christian or other religious-ethical values. This is why the realization of those principles in the Church's life as a witness to the world must always be the Church's priority. But we should also remember that in some cases, such as sexual and material equality, the Church has had to be reminded of biblical principles by other people's witness to them.

Permanent Norms and Cultural Relativity

If the fundamentals of the human situation have not changed since biblical times, the conditions and forms of human society have— drastically. In modern society, whether democratic or totalitarian, industrialized or already moving towards the coming post-industrialized situation, government is a very different business from what it was for Deborah, Hezekiah or Pontius Pilate. Both its methods and its functions have necessarily changed and continue to change. This must be kept at the forefront of our minds in all attempts to make political use of the Bible. Otherwise naive absurdities will result. To argue, for example, that since education in biblical times was not a government responsibility it should nowadays be left purely to parental responsibility, as it was then, makes no more sense than to argue that in accordance with biblical precedent governments should not legislate for road safety. The functions of government are much more extensive now than in biblical times, not because governments have overstepped the biblically defined limits of their authority, but because of the vastly increased complexity of modern society. This at the same time makes different, more democratic forms of government both more practicable and more desirable than in ancient societies.

We need, therefore, to take a thoroughly historical attitude to this matter. The functions and forms of government are highly changeable features of human life (by their very nature they must be), and the Bible cannot therefore provide rigid norms for political institutions and methods in all periods of history. Moreover, a recognition of this is not foreign to the Bible's own view of government. Genesis does not, as we might expect, trace the exercise of political authority back to creation or the Fall, but

10

describes its emergence in the course of the historical development of human culture. Just as cities (Gen. 4.17), music (Gen. 4.21) and viticulture (Gen. 9.20) did not descend from heaven, but had thoroughly human origins, so government, in its most common Old Testament form of kingship, emerged with Nimrod: 'the first on earth to be a mighty man' (Gen. 10.8).[1] The portrayal of Nimrod as a hunter (Gen. 10.9), and as ruling an empire formed not by conquest but by colonization (Gen. 10.10–12), is significant, since it links Nimrod's rule with the human task of dominion on earth as given by God, after the Flood, to Noah (Gen. 9.1–7). This task was not in itself necessarily political, but took political form in Nimrod, who as a hunter protected his people from wild animals (cf. Gen. 9.2, 5) and as founder of a colonial empire fulfilled the command to fill the earth (Gen. 9.1). Thus according to Genesis, kingship, the rule of one man over a whole society, originated as a way of fulfilling these God-given human tasks, even if, as the beginning of Nimrod's empire in Babel indicates (Gen. 10.10; cf. 11.1–9), it may not have been an ideal way of fulfilling them. But it is then very important to notice that the functions of Nimrod's rule, which account for the origin of kingship, were *not* the functions of government as Old Testament Israel knew government in later periods. Nimrod's fame as a hunter (Gen. 10.9) preserves a memory of a very early period of human society, when one of the special duties of a king was to ward off and destroy the wild animals threatening his community. In the historical period of the Old Testament this original function of kingship was preserved in a purely conventional form: hunting was the favourite sport of kings in Egypt and Mesopotamia. But the king's hunting no longer had the vital, practical function of preserving the life of the community. Nor was the colonizing of uninhabited land a major function of government in the time of Old Testament Israel. Thus the functions of Nimrod's kingship were no longer the functions of kingship when Genesis was written. By describing in this form the origins of government, Genesis recognizes the thoroughly historical character of human government, how its functions must change and develop in relation to the changes and development of human society. Legitimate government must always reflect God's will for human life, as Nimrod's did the divine command to Noah, and the Bible's account of God's will for human life will therefore always be relevant to it, but *how* it reflects God's will for human life, and what aspects of that will can appropriately be furthered by political institutions and methods, must change and can be discerned only in each new historical situation.

So we need to recognize that the political material in the Bible consists largely of stories about and instructions addressed to political societies very different from our own. I have sometimes wondered whether this is not part of the reason for the relatively modern tendency for many Christians to disengage from political and social reality. The adaptations needed to transfer biblical teaching on personal morality from its cultural situation to ours are comparatively easily made, but a more imaginative and creative hermeneutic is necessary for the Bible to speak to modern political life. Even when superficial parallels do strike us they can be highly problematic, as I discovered when leading studies on Joshua in a church house group at the time of the Israeli invasion of Lebanon.

The dilemma with which cultural relativity presents us is that the more specific the biblical material is in its application to its own historical context, the less relevant it seems to be in our context. Must we then look in the Bible only for permanent norms of a highly generalized character? This would be foreign to the nature of the Bible and would leave a great deal of it unusable, since the Bible is God's message in, to and through very particular historical situations. Its universality must be found *in and through* its particularity, not by peeling its particularity away until only a hard core of universality remains. So the appropriate method seems to be that of appreciating the biblical material first of all in its own culturally specific uniqueness, and then seeing it as a 'paradigm' (as Chris Wright suggests[2]) or an 'analogy' (as André Dumas suggests[3]) for our own time. In other words, the Bible provides models of God's purposes at work in particular political situations which can help us to discover and to implement his purposes in other situations. Such models, *because* they are highly specific, can often stimulate our thinking and imagination more effectively than very general principles can. For example, the law of gleaning in Leviticus 19.9–10 was appropriate only for a simple, agrarian society, but by observing how very appropriate it was as a means of provision for the poor in that society, we can be stimulated to think about forms of social legislation appropriate to our society. Of course we need always to consider such models in conjunction with the general principles that the Bible also provides. However, the principles are fairly general and the models cannot

12

be blueprints. In a sense they leave us considerable freedom to work out for ourselves, under the guidance of the Spirit, how God's purposes for human life can be realized in our political life. But that is rather a negative way of putting it. Positively, they can *inspire* our own creative thinking about politics today.

That the Bible's teaching is culturally specific, in the sense that it addresses specific situations in ancient history, will be generally acknowledged. Rather more controversial is the claim that the Bible's political teaching is in some degree *conditioned* by the social and political context in which it arose. But it seems to me we must recognize this as part of the real humanity of Scripture. For example, the political wisdom of the book of Proverbs, with its emphasis on the stability of a fixed social order (Prov. 19.10; 30.21−3) and its sometimes deferentially uncritical attitude to the monarchy (Prov. 16.10−15; 25.3), reflects the outlook of the court circles from which it derives. This makes it not a mistaken but a *limited* viewpoint, and therefore one which needs to be balanced by other aspects of biblical teaching. In this case at least, the relativizing effect of its cultural background coincides with the relativizing effect of its occupying its particular place in the whole canon of Scripture. We shall have more to say about the hermeneutical significance of the canon shortly.

Text and Context

Finally, we turn to the principles involved in reading a biblical text within the relevant contexts for its correct understanding. Inevitably we shall be mainly concerned with general principles that apply to all biblical interpretation, but we shall bear in mind the particular needs of political interpretation.

The meaning of a text is dependent on its context. This is the key to all responsible interpretation of biblical texts. But 'context' has a variety of aspects:

1. There is *the linguistic context* of accepted meanings of words and idioms in the linguistic milieu in which the text was written and first read.

2. There is *the immediate literary context* of the literary unit in which the text belongs. (The unit will often be the biblical book of which the text is now part, e.g. Mark's Gospel, but it may sometimes be a smaller unit, e.g. a psalm, and sometimes a larger unit, e.g. 1−2 Chronicles.)

3. There is *the wider literary context* of literary genre, conventions, allusions and so on, within the tradition of literature to which the text belongs.

4. There is *the cultural context* of the kind of society—political, social, economic, religious—in which the text originated.

5. There is *the broad historical context* of current events which may be relevant to understanding the text.

6. There is *the immediate historical context* in the life of the writer or his circle which occasioned the text.

All these aspects belong to the 'original' context in which the text was written. But a text which goes on being read and valued long after it was written acquires new contexts. In the case of a biblical text, its original literary unit has been incorporated into several larger literary contexts. A psalm, for example, which may originally have been an isolated literary unit, became part of one of the smaller collections of psalms which were then put together to make our psalter. In the process it may have been edited, to make it suitable for use in the temple when the collection was made, and may have been given a title. Then the psalter itself became part of the Hebrew canon of Scripture, and that in turn part of the Christian Bible, in which the psalm may be quoted and interpreted by New Testament writers. Each of these broader literary contexts must affect its meaning.

Then there are the constantly changing historical, cultural, liturgical and theological contexts within which the psalm has been read and understood down to the present day, some of which still affect our reading of it. Its meaning for us depends, then, on its original context (so far as we may be aware of it), on its wider literary contexts in the canon (so far as we take these into account), on traditional contexts (such as its interpretation in a particular theological tradition or its traditional place in a liturgy) which may influence our understanding of it, and on the contemporary context within which we read it. What this contemporary context amounts to depends, of course, on the interpreter's particular relationships to the world in which he lives.

Evidently the meaning of a text must change as it is read in these various new contexts. It will lose dimensions of meaning which it had in its original context (since aspects of that context have been lost or forgotten) and it will gain new dimensions of meaning as it acquires new contexts. Nevertheless the task of interpretation must presuppose that a constant (or at least recoverable) core of meaning persists and generates, in interaction with its new contexts, these new dimensions of meaning. Those who argue that the original context is irrelevant to a text's meaning for us should, logically, abandon the use of dictionaries and treat the Hebrew and Greek texts as mere meaningless marks on the page, to which they can give any meaning the shapes suggest to them! The historical nature of language itself requires us to give the original context a determinative role in the text's meaning for us. On the other hand, those who claim that a biblical text can legitimately mean only what it meant to its first readers need to be reminded of the way in which all great literature constantly transcends its original context and achieves fresh relevance to new situations.

Expanding Meaning

A brief example (not irrelevant to politics) may illustrate the way a biblical text can acquire new dimensions of meaning. Humanity's God-given dominion over the rest of the animals (Gen. 1.26, 28) must, for its first readers, have had a fairly restricted meaning, referring to their taming, hunting and farming of animals. In fact in Old Testament times the language of Genesis 1.26, which speaks of human dominion over all animals, must have seemed hyperbolic to anyone who thought about it, since many animals were not, in any realistic sense, under human dominion. (The writer of Job 39.2 – 12 certainly realized this.) In the context of its own literary unit, the book of Genesis, the text receives a kind of exposition in the account of Noah's relations with the animals, which again suggests a more far-reaching dominion than was the actual experience of Old Testament people. Then in the context of the Hebrew Bible, the thought of Genesis 1.26 is made, in Psalm 8.4 – 8, the basis for praise of God ('What is man that thou art mindful of him? . . . Yet thou hast made him little less than God'), with the implication that human dominion over the animals is to be exercised to the glory of God. The New Testament passage Hebrews 2.8 then gives the idea a christological significance, seeing Jesus as the man who will fully realize the ideal of human dominion over creation.

Both of these inner-canonical interpretations are relevant to the fresh extension of meaning which Genesis 1.26 has gained in our own time, when humanity has become so dominant as to threaten the very survival of much of the animal creation. Applying the text to this new situation, which could not have been envisaged by its author, is not a distortion, but a natural extension, of the text's 'core' meaning. Indeed, the open-ended language of the text really comes into its own only in modern times, when at last it is literally true that scarcely a species on earth can escape the effects of human activities. In this new situation it is clear that humanity, in its dominance on earth, incurs new responsibilities, such as the preservation of endangered species, which the first readers of Genesis 1.26, because of the restricted realization of their dominion, did not have. But precisely in this new situation, continuity with the original meaning of the text gains fresh importance, since this ensures that 'dominion' refers to responsible, not exploitative, rule, on the model of God's own care for his creation. I am surprised that Noah has not become, as he deserves to be, a model for Christian conservationists!

If a biblical text is not to mean whatever we want it to mean, we must pay disciplined attention to its original and canonical contexts. But if it is to mean something for us, we must pay equally disciplined attention to the contemporary context in which we interpret it.

Pre-Canonical Contexts

The term 'pre-canonical contexts' is really preferable to 'original context', because, as the example of a psalm (given above) illustrates, many biblical passages in fact passed through a series of historical contexts before entering the canon. Much biblical material existed first as oral tradition and/or passed through several stages of written compilation and editing before reaching its present form. The 'original' context is not always discoverable nor always the most important for our understanding of the text. To understand a psalm as originally composed may be less important than to understand it as part of the collection of temple hymns. A good rule of thumb (not to be applied without exceptions) is to take the present form of a biblical book as the primary context for exegesis, but to take account of the previous history of the materials contained in it in so far as these earlier contexts remain significant for understanding the material in the context of the biblical book. For example, the prophetic books of the Old Testament are edited collections of prophetic oracles, intended as such not for the prophet's contemporaries but for later readers.

But the relevance of the original context of these oracles is preserved within their later context, because the very nature of the oracles, which are often dated and address identifiable historical situations at the time of utterance, makes it impossible to ignore their original context.

To interpret the text in its pre-canonical contexts, the well-known methods of historical exegesis apply and must be rigorously applied. No exceptions must be allowed to the principle that the historical meaning of the text must be a meaning which readers at that time could perceive. Since the 'core meaning' of the text, which persists in all new contexts, must be contained in this historical meaning, this principle gives the task of achieving relative objectivity in historical exegesis a key role in preserving all interpretation from uncontrolled subjectivity. All new dimensions of meaning which a text may later acquire must be intelligibly continuous with a meaning accessible to readers of the text in its pre-canonical contexts.

Thus, for example, the medieval political exegesis of Luke 22.38, according to which the two swords represent the ecclesiastical and civil authorities of Christendom, is unacceptable because it has no basis in a meaning which could have been discovered by the first readers of the text.

The Canonical Context

The final context which is *authoritative* for the meaning of a biblical text is the complete canon of Scripture. We cannot be content to read a text as its pre-canonical readers read it, but must also read it in the context of the whole biblical story of God's dealings with his people and the overriding theological and moral themes of the Bible. This does not mean a harmonistic levelling out of the diversity and distinctiveness of the various parts of Scripture, because the canonical context is not a substitute for, but is additional to the pre-canonical contexts. It does mean that we must think about the relative significance of the various parts of the canon, and recognize that some viewpoints within Scripture are relativized or even corrected by others. It means appreciating that the unity of the canon sometimes emerges in dialectical fashion from the diversity of the canon. It involves us in constant interaction between understanding particular texts in their primary contexts and attempting a biblical theology which does justice to the whole canon.

The Contemporary Context

There are several dangers involved in the task of interpreting the text in the context of our contemporary world. One is the danger of manipulating the text to support our preconceived attitudes and projects. This is an often unconscious temptation in the political use of the Bible, since biblical authority can sometimes be a very useful source of justification for political policies and since we often find it difficult to be self-critical about our own political attitudes. To allow the Bible to challenge and change our political attitudes is harder than we perhaps realize.

Disciplined listening to the text in its original and canonical contexts is one protection against this danger. Of course, historical exegesis is never *wholly* objective, but the rigorous attempt at historical objectivity can liberate us from all kinds of misuse of the text. So can serious attention to the place of the text within the canon. Ideological abuse of Romans 13.1−7 to support the status quo can be corrected by reference to passages critical of unjust government. Study of the history of interpretation can also be helpful, since historical distance enables us to appreciate what was going on in the Church's political use of the Bible in the past more easily than we can in the present. For example, the nineteenth-century use of the Bible to justify slavery, even by so eminent a theologian as Charles Hodge,[4] is a salutary warning, which needs to be heeded especially where the interests of the interpreter's own class or nation are at stake in the interpretation of Scripture.

The peril of blindness to the influence of our interests on interpretation can also be countered by attention to the work of interpreters whose political and economic circumstances are different from our own. American black slaves read the Bible very differently from the way their masters read it. Today it is important that we listen to the liberation theologians of the Third World and that we try to hear how the Bible sounds to Christians persecuted by oppressive regimes. Of course we must recognize that revolutionary interpretations of Scripture can be as ideological as interpretations by those in power, just as feminist interpretations can be as ideological as patriarchal interpretations. But we have a duty to listen to anyone who claims that the Bible has been misused against them and to anyone whose interpretation of Scripture goes hand in hand with costly discipleship of Christ.

All this reminds us that in the end the task of contextualizing

Scripture today is the task of the whole Church, and must take place in the dialogue between Christians whose varied cultures, conditions and Christian traditions can alert them to aspects of Scripture which others may miss. Much discussion of contextualization has been about the different forms which Christianity should take within particular cultures today, and of course this is important. But at a time when the most urgent political issues are the international ones affecting all parts of the world, our political use of the Bible needs to reflect the thinking of the universal Church.

Another danger in relating the Bible to contemporary situations is that of too simplistic application. There are two antidotes to this. One is, again, careful study of the texts in their historical context, which will alert us to the real differences between that context and the modern one. Second, the more we realize how biblical texts relate to the actual social structures and economic conditions of their time, the more we shall see the need to engage in serious analysis of our contemporary world if we are to specify the Bible's relevance to it. Too often Christians concerned about social justice have imagined that Amos's critique of eighth-century Israel needs only a little adjustment to apply to our own society. But this is often cheap relevance, which evades the need for proper analysis of and prophetic insight into the actual evils of our society.

This last observation prompts us to notice, finally, that the Bible's meaning for today cannot result automatically from the correct use of a set of hermeneutical principles. It requires in the interpreters qualities of insight, imagination, critical judgement, and expert knowledge of the contemporary world. It also requires the guidance of the Holy Spirit, who inspired not the mere text but the contextual meaning of the text, and therefore remains active at the interface between the text and its changing contexts.

2: Holiness for the People

Leviticus 19

Leviticus 19 (RSV)

1, 2   And the LORD said to Moses, 'Say to all the congregation of
the people of Israel, You shall be holy; for I the LORD your
3   God am holy. Every one of you shall revere his mother and
4   his father, and you shall keep my sabbaths: I am the LORD
your God. Do not turn to idols or make for yourselves
molten gods: I am the LORD your God.

5   'When you offer a sacrifice of peace offerings to the
6   LORD, you shall offer it so that you may be accepted. It
shall be eaten the same day you offer it, or on the morrow;
and anything left over until the third day shall be burned
7   with fire. If it is eaten at all on the third day, it is an
8   abomination; it will not be accepted, and every one who
eats it shall bear his iniquity, because he has profaned a
holy thing of the LORD; and that person shall be cut off
from his people.

9   'When you reap the harvest of your land, you shall not
reap your field to its very border, neither shall you gather
10   the gleanings after your harvest. And you shall not strip
your vineyard bare, neither shall you gather the fallen
grapes of your vineyard; you shall leave them for the poor
and for the sojourner: I am the LORD your God.

11   'You shall not steal, nor deal falsely, nor lie to one
12   another. And you shall not swear by my name falsely, and
so profane the name of the LORD your God: I am the LORD.

13   'You shall not oppress your neighbour or rob him. The
wages of a hired servant shall not remain with you all night
14   until the morning. You shall not curse the deaf or put a
stumbling block before the blind, but you shall fear your
God: I am the LORD.

15   'You shall do no injustice in judgment; you shall not be
partial to the poor or defer to the great, but in righteousness

16 shall you judge your neighbour. You shall not go up and down as a slanderer among your people, and you shall not stand forth against the life of your neighbour: I am the LORD.

17 'You shall not hate your brother in your heart, but you shall reason with your neighbour, lest you bear sin because

18 of him. You shall not take vengeance or bear any grudge against the sons of your own people, but you shall love your neighbour as yourself: I am the LORD.

19 'You shall keep my statutes. You shall not let your cattle breed with a different kind; you shall not sow your field with two kinds of seed; nor shall there come upon you a garment of cloth made of two kinds of stuff.

20 'If a man lies carnally with a woman who is a slave, betrothed to another man and not yet ransomed or given her

21 freedom, an inquiry shall be held. They shall not be put to death, because she was not free; but he shall bring a guilt offering for himself to the LORD, to the door of the tent of

22 meeting, a ram for a guilt offering. And the priest shall make atonement for him with the ram of the guilt offering before the LORD for his sin which he has committed; and the sin which he has committed shall be forgiven him.

23 'When you come into the land and plant all kinds of trees for food, then you shall count their fruit as forbidden; three

24 years it shall be forbidden to you, it must not be eaten. And in the fourth year all their fruit shall be holy, an offering of

25 praise to the LORD. But in the fifth year you may eat of their fruit, that they may yield more richly for you: I am the LORD your God.

26 'You shall not eat any flesh with the blood in it. You shall

27 not practise augury or witchcraft. You shall not round off the hair on your temples or mar the edges of your beard.

28 You shall not make any cuttings in your flesh on account of the dead or tattoo any marks upon you: I am the LORD.

29 'Do not profane your daughter by making her a harlot, lest the land fall into harlotry and the land become full of

30 wickedness. You shall keep my sabbaths and reverence my sanctuary: I am the LORD.

31 'Do not turn to mediums or wizards; do not seek them out, to be defiled by them: I am the LORD your God.

21

32   'You shall rise up before the hoary head, and honour the
        face of an old man, and you shall fear your God: I am the
        LORD.
33   'When a stranger sojourns with you in your land, you
34   shall not do him wrong. The stranger who sojourns with
        you shall be to you as the native among you, and you shall
        love him as yourself; for you were strangers in the land of
        Egypt: I am the LORD your God.
35   'You shall do no wrong in judgment, in measures of
36   length or weight or quantity. You shall have just balances,
        just weights, a just ephah, and a just hin: I am the LORD
        your God, who brought you out of the land of Egypt.
37   'And you shall observe all my statutes and all my ordin-
        ances, and do them: I am the LORD.'

Introduction

Leviticus 19 will serve to illustrate many of the issues involved in
considering the modern political relevance of Old Testament law.
It occupies a rather special place within Leviticus, though the
casual reader may not immediately discern this. He will notice, no
doubt, that the sacrificial and other cultic concerns which occupy
most of Leviticus are less prominent in this chapter, though not
absent from it. But he will also gain the impression of a fairly
random collection of miscellaneous commands, ranging from the
very general to the incongruously specific. As far as modern
relevance is concerned, he may be encouraged, reading verses
13–18, to consider this obvious and straightforward, but will
then be brought up short as the command to love one's neighbour
(v. 18b) is followed at once by the taboo against mixing different
kinds of things (v. 19) and the ruling about the case of a man who
sleeps with a betrothed slave-girl (vv. 20–2), where not only is
the circumstance alien to our culture but the legal rationale hard to
understand.

Principles and Illustrations

The key to the chapter is its introduction in verse 2 ('You shall be
holy; for I the LORD your God am holy'), along with the repetition
of 'I am the LORD your God' or 'I am the LORD' after most of the
laws (vv. 3, 4, 10, 11, 14, 16, 18, 25, 28, 30, 31, 32, 34, 36) and
after the summarizing conclusion (v. 37). The introduction, which
forms a kind of motto for the theology of Leviticus (cf. Lev.

11.44−5; 20.26), refers to Israel as the covenant people of God, bound to him in a special relationship of holiness. To be holy means, fundamentally, to be set apart. God has pledged himself to be, in a special sense, Israel's God, and in consequence Israel is set apart from the other nations as God's own people (cf. Lev. 20.26, for this meaning of holiness). The introduction could be paraphrased, 'You shall be my people and mine alone, for I am your God and yours alone.'[1] Israel's special status as God's covenant people, whom he has dedicated to himself, is also a calling to be lived out in a life dedicated to God. That this is the point of all the laws is then indicated by the refrain, 'I am the LORD your God,' which indicates that these laws are what the covenant God demands of his people (for the significance of the refrain, cf. especially Lev. 22.31−3).

The theme of the chapter, then, is the holiness of the people of God in the whole of their life as a people belonging to him. This holiness consists both in what we might distinguish (though Leviticus itself does not) as cultic holiness−the concept, strange to most of us, of times, places and things set apart as God's (vv. 5−8, 23−5, 30)−and moral holiness, exemplified here in the provision for social love and justice. The fact that holiness is intended to characterize the whole of Israel's life accounts for the miscellaneous character of the chapter. Alongside some very general principles (e.g. vv. 11a, 18b, 30), some very specific examples (e.g. 20−2, 27−8) are included as *illustrations* of the way in which holiness should be lived out in the whole of Israel's life. The element of randomness, in other words, has a representative character. Aspects of holiness which are treated more fully elsewhere in Leviticus are represented here by specific illustrations: sacrifices (vv. 5−8), judicial case law (vv. 20−3), festivals (vv. 3b, 30a), economic obligations to God (vv. 23−5). The chapter majors on social morality (vv. 9−18, 32−6), giving in this area both general principles and detailed illustrations, but social morality is integrated into a picture of Israel's holiness in every aspect of her life.

Another general feature of the chapter which is worth noticing at this point is its relationship to the Decalogue. Most of the ten commandments appear in some form in Leviticus 19:[2]

I   v. 4a

II   v. 4

III v. 12

IV   vv. 3b, 30
V   v. 3a
VI   cf. v. 16b
VII cf. vv. 20−2
VIII vv. 11a, 13, 35−6
IX   v. 16
X

Some of the parallels are very exact. In some cases only an instance of the topic covered by the Decalogue commandment occurs. Thus v. 16b refers to only one, though an important, category of murder: using false charges in court to secure an enemy's judicial execution. Sexual offences (the realm of the seventh commandment) are dealt with extensively elsewhere in Leviticus and are represented here only by the case of vv. 20−22, which illustrates the problem of defining adultery in legal and moral terms. Only the tenth commandment−against coveting−is completely unrepresented in Leviticus 19, but the special character of this commandment among the ten, its reference to intention as well as action, is paralleled here by vv. 17−18.

The chapter's relationship to the Decalogue illustrates the way in which the Decalogue crystallizes general principles at the heart of the whole Law. The general principles of the Decalogue appear here both explicitly as stated principles (e.g. v. 11a) and implicitly as the principles behind more specific applications of them (e.g. vv. 35−36). Moreover the Decalogue itself covers the same broad range of subject-matter as this chapter: religious obligation, cultic holiness, social and family ethics.

To realise that the law works with general principles, which are sometimes stated explicitly and sometimes remain implicit in more specific commandments, is very important. This chapter contains other general principles besides those of the Decalogue. The love commandment (vv. 18b, 34) is one very general principle, which is explicitly stated and to which we shall return. A general principle which remains implicit is that of special concern for the underprivileged: a principle which lies behind specific command-ments here (vv. 9−10, 13b, 14, 33−34) and many other parts of the Old Testament Law. Another is the principle of avoiding the religious practices of the Canaanites, which is explicit in 20.23 and implicit in specific commandments of this chapter (vv. 26−29, 31). Identifying general principles is important because the real purpose of the Law is to inculcate general principles and values and to teach people to apply them in specific instances. This is done by stating general principles and by illustrating, with specific examples, how general principles can be applied in specific cases. The method is formally not unlike that of Jesus in the Sermon on the Mount, where, for example, the general principle, 'Do not resist one who is evil' (Matt. 5:39a) is illustrated by specific examples of what this would mean (vv. 39b—42). There are differences—for example, Jesus chooses deliberately extreme examples to illustrate his point—but the basic similarity is instructive. The difference between the Law and the teaching of Jesus is not that the Law regulates every detail of life and Jesus gives only general principles of morality. In both cases general principles are *illustrated* by specific examples, because without such examples people could never learn how general principles apply in specific cases. But the Law, no more than Jesus, provides exhaustive rules for all specific cases. It may provide more numerous specific rules, but they are still only *illustrations*, designed to educate people in the spirit of the Law, so that they will learn by analogy how to behave in cases the Law does not mention.

So far we have spoken of law in terms of religious obligations, cultic rules, and social morality, not in terms of judicial law, intended to be enforced in the courts. This kind of law, which prescribes penalties for particular cases, is represented in Leviticus 19 only by vv. 20—22, and even this law prescribes a cultic action (sacrifice). The law courts are also in view in vv. 12, 15—16, but these verses are not themselves judicial laws for the courts to administer: they are ethical prescriptions for the way judges and plaintiffs should conduct themselves in court proceedings. Thus the chapter is concerned to show that the holiness required of the people of God has implications for the administration of justice, as one area of Israel's life, but it is not itself a law-code for the courts to administer. As a further indication of this, it should be noted that the chapter covers offences, notably theft (vv. 11, 13), which were certainly subject to prosecution and punishment in the courts, but it deals with them in the form of moral admonitions, not in the form of laws to be applied by the courts. One needs only to compare the case laws on theft in Exodus 22.1—8 to see the difference. In the case of some of the actions prohibited in Leviticus

19 (vv. 9−10, 13b), we cannot be sure whether or not they were punishable by the courts, though it seems improbable that they were. But in any case the authority of the covenant God (indicated by the formula 'I am the LORD') is sufficient sanction for this chapter's purposes.

Of course elsewhere the Pentateuch does include a good many criminal and civil laws which could be used in the administration of justice in the courts. But two observations need to be made on this. In the first place they are embedded in contexts which also include alongside them moral exhortations, general moral principles, cultic rules, and so on. Second, they are not sufficient to form a code of law for regular consultation by the judicial authorities. They are *examples* of laws rather than an exhaustive collection. Thus the place of judicial laws in the whole corpus of Old Testament law is not entirely unlike that of verses 20−2 in chapter 19 of Leviticus. Neither the Old Testament law as a whole, nor specific parts of it, should be regarded as a statute-book for use in the courts. Rather its purpose is to educate the people of God in the will of God for the whole of their life as his people, to create and develop the conscience of the community. It instructs the whole people in the values and principles of their social order, and as part of this instruction includes representative examples of the kind of laws which should be administered in the courts. These could be regarded as 'exercises' in legal thinking, both for judges and for the community as a whole. By familiarizing themselves with these paradigm laws, they could learn how to apply the general principles of God's law in specific judicial cases.[3]

Old Testament Law and Modern Society

In considering what kind of relevance Old Testament law might have for modern political society, it is important to remember the point which emerges rather clearly in Leviticus 19: that the law was intended to promote the holiness of the covenant people of God in every area of their life. It is not concerned to distinguish aspects of God's will for his people which are subject to legal enforcement or political action and those which are not. Cultic obligations, social morality, personal morality, judicial law are promiscuously mixed, and the overriding concern is with obedience to God in the whole of life. In other words, it is addressed to a theocratic society: a religious community which is also a political entity. Retrospectively, we may attempt to make distinctions between various categories of law, but such distinctions are not easy to make. The traditional Christian division of the Old Testament law into ceremonial, civil and moral has only a limited usefulness. In particular, it correctly recognizes that the category of cultic holiness, which governs the law's distinctions between the holy, the clean, and the unclean, has been rendered obsolete for Christians by the New Testament, which consistently translates such notions into matters of moral holiness. But this does not mean that the cultic provisions of Old Testament law can always be neatly disentangled from its other aspects: in Leviticus 19.20−2 a civil law and a cultic practice are inseparable.

More problematic is the traditional distinction between moral law and civil law. The law, as we have seen, is concerned with broad principles of social morality and with illustrating their specific application. The specific examples include both laws enforceable in the courts and moral exhortations. Leviticus 19.9−10 is not in the form of judicial law and, we may guess, would not normally have been enforced in the courts. But on the other hand, it would have been open to the elders in any particular local community to choose to enforce it with legal sanctions. In any case it had the force of social custom, which in small, close-knit communities like those of ancient Israel can be very effective. In such a society, social disapproval, which itself is inseparable from shared religious beliefs, can be as important a sanction as legal punishment. Thus to insist that these verses envisage private charity rather than state welfare—or vice versa—is to introduce anachronistic distinctions. Moreover, as this example illustrates, the distinction between moral and civil law scarcely helps us with the problem of modern relevance. Whether we consider it moral or civil law, Leviticus 19.9−10 is a *culturally specific* law. It was an effective means of provision for the poor in the economic circumstances of ancient Israel, but would not be in modern Britain, where, on the one hand, most people are not farmers, and, on the other hand, the majority of the poor, who live in the inner cities, will not be much helped by the food they could gather on country rambles. The relevance of this law for us can be discovered only by discerning the principles at work in it. How far these principles can or should be embodied in social legislation in our society, rather than being matters of purely voluntary social morality, is something we have to decide in the concrete circumstances of our own society. No attempt to distinguish between moral law and civil law in ancient Israel will help us there.

However, the problems of application are not yet solved by the decision to look for general principles. We will continue to use Leviticus 19.9–10 as an example. No doubt the right of poor people to glean was not created by the law, but was an old-established custom which the law accepts and approves. The law is concerned with protecting the value of this right against the self-interested efficiency of farmers who will be tempted to leave as little as possible for the poor to glean. This concern can be seen to arise from two broad principles of the law. One is the need to provide for those who have no economic resources of their own (cf. Exod. 23.10–11; Deut. 14.28–9; 23.24–5). This is itself an implication of the most general social principle of Leviticus 19: 'you shall love your neighbour as yourself' (v. 18b). If other people deserve the same consideration as one gives oneself, then those who do not have the means of supporting themselves have a right to some of the surplus of those who do. In an agrarian society in which the norm was that every family owned land, the few who did not deserved a right to some of the produce of those who did. But a second principle is also operative: that Israelite landowners were really only tenants of the land which belonged to God (Lev. 25.23). And since God gave the land to his people for the support of all the people, no individual landowner had an absolute right to the produce of his land. His duty to support the poor was a consequence of his acknowledgement that he held his land in trust from God. It was this religious principle of Israel's covenant relationship with God which qualified the rights of landowners in Israel and made private ownership of land acceptable only in close connection with public responsibility for the landless.[4] We can see this more obviously when the law of Leviticus 19.9–10 is repeated in Leviticus 23.22 in the context of the laws for cultic festivals. There it follows the rules for one of Israel's harvest festivals: the wheat harvest (Pentecost). The thankful acknowledgement, in the festival, that the land and its produce are given by God finds another necessary expression in leaving the gleanings for the poor.

Thus the attempt to discern general principles brings us back to the holistic nature of the law, in which the religious and the social

28

cannot be separated and everything is rooted in Israel's relationship to her God. If Israel, as envisaged by the law, provides in some sense a model for societies as God intends them to be, it is a model which seems to point towards theocratic societies in which the religious and political communities coincide. But the theocratic ideal, as we know both from the history of Israel herself and from the history of Christendom, usually betrays itself in application. It founders on the tension between the high degree of voluntary religious commitment which it requires (and for which the Old Testament law constantly calls) and the involuntary nature of membership of a political community. This tension can only be resolved in the eschatological Kingdom of God, in which the theocratic ideal towards which the law points will be fulfilled. Between Old Testament Israel and the eschatological Kingdom there lie two forms of society in which the Kingdom is only partially and in different ways anticipated: the Church and the state. The Church, because it is a voluntary, not a political, community, ought to be able to live out the religious and moral demands of God in relationship to him *more* fully than Old Testament Israel could. It will live them out as a society, but not as a political entity. Therefore the extent to which Israel, as envisaged in the law, provides a model for the *Church* must be qualified: the specifically political element in the model finds no realization in the Church. On the other hand, the norms for human life in political society which are expressed in the Old Testament law can to some degree be realized in other political societies. But this realization will be qualified by the fact that no political society, however much influenced by biblical faith, manifests, as a political society, the kind of wholehearted commitment to the God of Israel that the law demands.

Thus we have a somewhat complex picture, in which the relevance of the Old Testament law to us cannot be understood apart from its and our place in the salvation history which leads from ancient Israel to the future Kingdom of God. The Old Testament law, in envisaging a political society living out the holiness of a people dedicated to God, points towards the eschatological Kingdom, when such a society will be universally realized. But it attempts to anticipate that ideal in the circumstances of ancient Near Eastern society, which requires not only cultural specificity but also compromise. The New Testament Church, as an international community without specifically political identity, is both continuous and discontinuous with Old Testament Israel. Like Israel, it is called to be a holy people dedicated to God in every aspect of its life, and so the motto of Leviticus (Lev. 19.2) is applied to the church in 1 Peter 1.15–16. The Church is intended to approximate to the eschatological ideal more closely both in its universal openness and in its dedication to radical holiness. But it can do this precisely because it is not a political entity, and so it must always resist the temptation to become one. At the same time its witness and commitment to the Kingdom of God in the political societies of which it is part must include the attempt to realize the values of the Kingdom of God in those societies as political societies. This attempt, like the Old Testament law, will involve both cultural specificity and compromise, but, unlike the Old Testament law, its presuppositions and its aims cannot be theocratic. It follows that both for the Church's own life as the people of God and for Christian political activity, the Old Testament law can be highly instructive, but it cannot be straightforward instructions. Its relevance needs careful assessment in each case.

The holistic nature of the Old Testament law forbids its simplistic application to modern secular, pluralistic societies. But this holistic character itself constitutes an important reminder that political structures, activity and legislation cannot be divorced from the values a political society has in common. Political policies and judicial laws presuppose and express moral values, and while they may play a role in forming the values generally accepted in society they cannot run too far ahead of the accepted norms and often depend for their effectiveness on other means of influencing the moral climate. Most laws are obeyed most of the time not just because people fear punishment, but because they accept that the laws are right and feel some degree of moral obligation to obey them. Thus the strategy of the Old Testament law, in seeking to educate the people in social norms and values, to form the conscience of the nation, and to set its examples of judicial law within that broader context, is not irrelevant to modern societies. The need for some such strategy raises difficult but very important questions in a pluralistic society where common values cannot be founded on commitment to a common religious or non-religious expression of ultimate values.

Finally, this means that the Church's political relevance is to be sought not only in specifically political activities. By attempting to

live out the values of the Kingdom of God in the Church's own life
as a community and as members of that community who also play
a full part in the rest of society, the Church influences, in countless
ways, the climate of values in society at large. As John Taylor,
writing of the 'biblical theology of enough', which he finds
exemplified in the law of gleaning, says: 'We are dealing with a
way of life which God's minority is called to take as its standard in
the midst of the world for the sake of God's majority. This is the
significance for us of this old Hebrew life-style.'[5]

Honouring Grey Hair

As an example of the continued relevance of Leviticus 19, we
select verse 32: 'You shall rise in the presence of grey hairs, give
honour to the aged, and fear your God' (NEB). This happens to be
an aspect of social ethics which the New Testament fails to
mention, and so it illustrates the fact that the New Testament
presupposes the Old rather than supersedes it.

Respect for the old is the extension, on a wider social scale, of
the fifth commandment of the Decalogue, which enjoins respect
for parents and appears in this chapter at verse 3a. We must
notice that respect for parents and for the old more generally had a
social function in ancient Israel which it does not have in our
society. Age conferred authority both within the extended family
and in the local community. The head of an extended family
exercised a legal authority over all his dependants, including
married sons and their families, and so performed functions which
in modern societies have passed to the state. The harsh treatment
of the rebellious son, prescribed in Deuteronomy 21.18—21, has
to be understood in this context: the offence is perceived as a
threat to the structure of authority in the community, and so the
civil law intervenes to maintain authority in the family. But also
beyond the context of the family, the 'elders' who acted as both a
local council and a local court were literally elders: the heads of
households who held office in the community by virtue of seniority.
Thus the respect due to the old, in ancient Israel, was in part the
respect due to the agents of law and government in that society.

If this were all it was, we might well consider Leviticus 19.32
irrelevant to our own society. But the injunction, 'fear your God',
which also accompanies the prohibition on taking advantage of
the handicapped in verse 14 (cf. also Lev. 25.17, 36, 43), indicates
that the main point in verse 32 is respect for old people who were

all too easily treated with contempt. They include those who are too frail in body or mind to exercise authority, those who in fact are past the age of being of any use in the community. Leviticus 27.1−7 gives a most interesting insight into the relative uselessness of the old as it was perceived in Israel. The prices at which people of various ages and sexes are there valued are presumably the rates which would be paid in the market if people were sold as slaves, and so reflect the general estimate of their usefulness in terms of productive labour.[6] Those over sixty are worth very much less than those in the prime of life. Thus contempt for the old, who had outlived their economic usefulness and had to be supported by the young, was a real temptation (cf. Isa. 3.5; Mic. 7.6; Prov. 30.17). Proverbs 28.24 refers to people who think it is no robbery to take over their dependent parents' possessions without permission.

Thus relationships between the generations in Israel were as complex as they are in any society. If the old enjoyed the dignity of authority in the community and were respected for their wisdom (Job 15.7−10; 32.6−7), as is characteristic of most traditional societies, they were also vulnerable, in weakness and senility, to contempt and mistreatment by the young.

It hardly needs to be said that respect for the old is much needed in our society, where they form an increasingly large proportion of the population. *Society*'s respect for the old can be implemented in political measures of various kinds: financing pensions, health care, social services, and encouragement of voluntary initiatives. Pensions, for example, ought to be such as to give proper recognition not only to the contribution which pensioners have given to the community during their working lives, but to the contributions which many continue to make. This needs to be stressed in a society which tends to overvalue paid employment by comparison with unpaid contributions to society, such as housework, raising children and voluntary service in the community. As more people take early retirement and more remain healthy and active longer, there need to be imaginative efforts to give roles in society to the 'post-employed'. The kinds of tasks appropriate to older people which they assumed fairly naturally in the Israelite extended family and family-based economy ought to be available, but often are not, in a society with a tendency, as ours has, to leave the old out of its major activities. Even in a rapidly changing society, where the young easily suppose they understand the contemporary world so much better than their elders, a lifetime's experience has much to offer.

However, it is not only the useful who deserve respect. Society must practise respect also for those who become helpless through physical weakness and—an increasing phenomenon as people survive longer—sink into senile dementia. Such respect is not easy for those who devote large parts of their lives to caring for frustratingly difficult and demanding elderly relatives, and so society must give financial and other kinds of support to those who care for the elderly at home, as well as providing institutional care for others. Leviticus 19.32—even in a society where extended families living in close proximity were the norm—enjoins respect, not only for parents by children, but for all old people by society as a whole.

However, such political actions are not sufficient to meet the problem of the widespread neglect and contempt of the old in our society, in which many old people who live alone are never visited by anyone, in which the old are often subject to vicious taunts and assaults by children and youths, in which there are estates where the old can live only in constant fear. This broader problem can be met only as respect for the old becomes once again a prevalent social value. Not only legal and institutional measures, but also the strategy of Leviticus 19 is needed: moral education or (since that term may suggest something too narrow, done only in schools) nurturing values.[7] Respect for the old conflicts with the youth-centred values of our society, and with the pursuit of a spurious kind of up-to-the-minute contemporaneity, promoted by commercial interests. It needs vigorous promotion. Admittedly, the task of nurturing common values in a pluralistic society has problems quite alien to the Israelite theocracy, but it also has opportunities of its own. Respect for the old has a prominent place among the cultural values of the Asian communities, and one might hope that instead of seeing it eroded in their contact with secular Britain they may help to promote it. It would be a pity if the Churches could not do so too.

When is Adultery not Adultery?

It would be misleading to leave the impression that all of the law is as applicable to modern society as Leviticus 19.32. As a very different example, we shall consider verses 20—2:

If a man sleeps with a slave-girl who has been assigned to another man, but not fully redeemed or given her freedom, damages must be paid.[8] They must not be put to death, because she was not free. He must bring his reparation to the Lord to the entrance of the tent of meeting, a ram as a reparation offering. The priest must make atonement for him before the Lord with the ram of the reparation offering because of the sin he committed, and he shall receive forgiveness for the sin he committed.[9]

Since we are not likely to think of implementing this law, it cannot mean anything at all to us unless we examine the legal thinking which is at work in it.[10] It envisages a problematic case: a case which would have been adultery if the woman had not been a slave. The woman is betrothed ('assigned to another man'), and for the purposes of the law a betrothed woman was treated as already married. If a man had sex with a woman betrothed to another and her consent could be assumed, both were subject to the death penalty (Deut. 22.23−4), just as in other cases of adultery (Lev. 20.10).[11] However, in this case the woman is a slave. She is going to receive her freedom, in order to be married as a free wife, but has not yet done so. A slave was the property of her master. She could not be a wife, in the full legal sense, only a concubine, and so adultery with her was, by definition, not possible. The problem in this case lies in the legally ambiguous status of the woman: she is betrothed to be married, but is still a slave.

The ruling given is that, as far as legal penalties go, the case cannot be considered adultery. So the death penalty is appropriate neither for the slave nor for her lover. Instead the lover must pay damages to her owner, since, in effect, he has reduced the value of his property. (Compare the compensation which the lover of an unmarried girl must pay to her father, according to Exodus 22.17.) The fact that the couple are spared the death penalty may seem merciful to us, but the *reason* for this is not mercy, but the fact that the law considers the girl a chattel, not a legal person.

However, the marginality of the case means that the law is not content with financial compensation to the owner, but prescribes that the offending man also offer compensation *to God* in the form of a 'reparation offering' (called in most translations a 'guilt offering'). This is the type of sacrifice prescribed in Leviticus

5.14—6.7 for atonement for sins against God's holiness. At first sight it might seem as though our case is being considered comparable with those property offences discussed in Leviticus 6.1—7, but the latter are not simply cases of robbing other people, for which reparation offerings would not be required: they are cases involving swearing falsely by God's name (Lev. 6.3, 5), and thus offences against God's holiness.[12] So it is not because our case involves damage to property that a reparation offering is prescribed. Rather it is because it is arguably a case of adultery. In Israel adultery, as a transgression of one of the fundamental laws of the covenant (Exod. 20.14), was an offence against the covenant God. This is why it was punishable by death. In the present case, because the offence was arguably not adultery, the death penalty was disallowed, but because, on the other hand, it *was* arguably adultery, a form of reparation to God, of a type required in cases of serious offence against God, was prescribed.[13]

The reader might be tempted to suppose that the law, while treating the girl as a slave in the eyes of society, maintains her status as a person in the eyes of God by prescribing the sacrifice. But this is not really the point. The sacrifice is required not because *any* slave is a person in the sight of God, but simply because *this* slave is betrothed, and this anomalous legal status makes the case neither clearly one of adultery nor clearly not one of adultery.

Only one aspect of this law distinguishes it from the kind of legal reasoning which was normal in the law codes of the ancient Near East. This is the principle that the law must treat adultery as a violation of Israel's covenant with her God.[14] But in its understanding of the legal implications of slavery, this law is indistinguishable from contemporary non-Israelite law. Other aspects of Old Testament law, it is true, considerably mitigate the condition of slaves, so that it might even be said that, while accepting the contemporary institution of slavery, the law at the same time undermines it. Slaves in Israel had legal rights which they did not have elsewhere.[15] Nevertheless, it is important to be reminded by the law we have studied that slaves certainly did not have equal status in Israelite law with free men and women.[16] Though the law does not consistently treat them as mere chattels, in cases such as this the operative principle is that they are not legal persons, but property.

We rightly find this unacceptable. The point is not so much that we deplore the effect of this particular law, which (if we take for granted the institution of slavery) did not operate to the disadvantage of the slave. The point is rather that the *principle* implicit in this law—that a slave does not have the same legal status as a free person—is unacceptable to us. In other words, slavery as such, which depends on this principle, is unacceptable to us, however humanely it may be operated.

'Israelite law (like any law) has to start where its own people are.'[17] Characteristically, Old Testament law adopts many of the principles and practices of its environment. Slavery, which was universal in the societies of the ancient Near East, was one of these. Such principles and practices were adapted under pressure of the principles of Israel's covenant relationship with her God, but imperfectly. Slavery was mitigated, but not abolished. Principles and practices which *we* can see to be inconsistent with the fundamental will of the biblical God remain stubbornly part of his law. Not that we can distinguish the ideal and the compromising within the law by distinguishing what was distinctively Israelite from what was common among Israel's neighbours. Many excellent features of the law, such as its concern for the disadvantaged, were shared with the laws of other societies.[18] Rather, we have to measure the laws of the Old Testament against the whole thrust of the biblical revelation of God's will. We shall see in chapter 7 how slavery then emerges as inconsistent with God's fundamental will.

The warrant for a discriminating treatment of Old Testament law is given by Jesus in his treatment of the law of divorce: 'For your hardness of heart Moses allowed you to divorce your wives, but from the beginning it was not so' (Matt. 19.8). Jesus here distinguishes God's fundamental will for human marriage from the laws which assume that, because of human sin, divorce will happen and therefore regulate and limit it. This is not a condemnation of Moses. Old Testament judicial law, in this and many other instances, did what the laws of political societies have to do: it brought fundamental moral principles to bear on the intractable realities of sinful human society. If it was to be effective in judicial practice, it had to start where its people were. We have to acknowledge, on the one hand, the same need for compromise in legislation today, but also, on the other hand, that the compromise will not necessarily be in the same areas or of the same kind. Israel's qualified acceptance of slavery has a specific

36

historical and cultural context. It does not mean that fallen human nature is such that slavery is bound to exist in all human societies in this world, as some of the Church Fathers concluded. To set limits in advance to the extent to which fundamental moral principles can affect the structures and practices of society as a whole is always dangerous, and, as in the case of slavery, can be disproved by history. Christian politicians need not only the compromising realism of Old Testament law, which, after all, experience teaches easily enough, but also the reforming direction of Old Testament law, which brought the fundamental will of Israel's God to bear on contemporary social practices. Old Testament law can be a model for us not as a static blueprint, but as a dynamic process whose direction we can follow, in some cases, beyond the point at which the law itself had to stop.

Jesus and Leviticus 19

To assist us in discerning and following the dynamic direction of the law, we shall note, finally, three aspects of Jesus' interpretation of laws in Leviticus 19.

Leviticus 19.12 applies the third commandment of the Decalogue ('You shall not take the name of the LORD your God in vain', Exod. 20.7) to the swearing of oaths in court: 'You shall not swear by my name falsely, and so profane the name of your God.' This is connected with stealing (as in Lev. 6.1—7), which is the subject in the context (vv. 11, 13), because in a court case involving property in which the evidence was inconclusive, testimony on oath would be used to settle the case.

Jesus refers to this law in Matthew 5.33—7: 'You have heard that it was said to the men of old, "You shall not swear falsely . . ." But I say to you, Do not swear at all . . . Let what you say be simply "Yes" or "No" . . .' (RSV; see also Jas. 5.12). This is a good example of the way in which Jesus identifies the underlying intention of the law and extends or intensifies its application. Leviticus 19 prohibits *false* oaths; Jesus prohibits *all* oaths. The point is that oaths are needed only because it cannot be assumed that people are truthful when not under oath. But Jesus takes the law's demand for truthfulness and extends it to a requirement of absolute truthfulness all the time. Those who are transparently truthful in all they say should not need to use oaths. Thus whereas the law makes a minimal demand for truthfulness *at least* under oath, Jesus makes a maximal demand for total truthfulness.

Jesus, as in all his ethical teaching, presses the fundamental intention of the law to the absolute limit, as the standard at which his followers must aim. It is in this sense that their righteousness should exceed the righteousness of those who are content to keep within the bounds of the letter of the Old Testament law (Matt. 5.20). Is it the implication of Jesus' teaching that we must dispense with the use of oaths in court? Only a utopian society could make the assumption that all its citizens are totally truthful people.[19] Therefore we still need the strategy of Leviticus's attempt to ensure that people at least tell the truth when giving evidence in court. But it does not follow that Jesus' demand for total truthfulness is relevant only to the personal ethics of his disciples. The dynamic of the law, which Jesus uncovers, is towards as much truthfulness as possible in public, as well as private, life. If people in public life find themselves having to assure the public, with some equivalent of an oath, that what they are saying on a particular occasion really is the honest truth, something is wrong with the general standard of truthfulness in public life. And the traditional Quaker abstention from all oaths, while from one point of view it was a rather too legalistic form of obedience to Jesus' teaching, has also served as a form of public witness to the need for truthfulness in all political and social relations.

Second, Jesus identified the command to love one's neighbour as oneself (Lev. 19.18b) as one of the two great commandments on which 'depend all the law and the prophets' (Matt. 22. 39—40). In other words it is the command which sums up all other duties towards our fellow men and women (see also Rom. 13.8—10). This, in fact, follows quite naturally from the place of the commandment in Leviticus 19. The literary structure of verses 11—18 gives verse 18b the character of a climax, which is not only the complement of verse 18a but also the summarizing principle of the whole passage.[20] Its reappearance in verse 34 confirms its status as the most basic principle of social relations, and if, as we have suggested, Leviticus 19 represents *in nuce* the whole range of the obligations of the law, then the love of one's neighbour as oneself is indeed the fundamental principle of all the law's commandments about relationship with neighbours. No other principles, not even those of the Decalogue (cf. Rom. 13.9), stand alongside this commandment as *additional* principles. All, in the end, are illustrative instances of it.

This does not make them unnecessary. They are needed in order to spell out what the love of neighbour involves.[21] But they are not exhaustive of it.[Loving one's neighbour as oneself always exceeds what any other laws can specify.]In political terms, this means that there are always new implications of social love to be discovered. Moreover, if the other commandments help to interpret the love commandment, it in turn must guide the interpretation of them. If it sums them all up, they cannot be rightly interpreted in a way inconsistent with it. Apparent biblical support for laws and policies which oppress and dehumanize people must always be spurious, and can always be refuted by reference to the love commandment. Finally, as the most basic intention of the Old Testament law, the love commandment provides the dynamic which in some cases must overtake other provisions of the law. In the case of slavery, for example, not only does it mitigate slavery within the law (e.g. Lev. 25.39—55). In the end, as the nineteenth-century abolitionists saw, it cannot tolerate the existence of slavery at all. If other people deserve the same consideration as I give myself, then we must have equal status in law.

Third, Jesus interpreted the commandment to love one's neighbour as including all human beings without exception. The 'neighbour' in Leviticus 19.18b—synonymous with 'brother', 'fellow countryman', and 'kinsman' in verses 11—18 (cf. NEB)—is a fellow Israelite, a fellow member of the covenant community. However, it is significant that Leviticus 19 itself extends the same principle to resident foreigners in verse 34: 'Let the resident alien among you be treated like one of yourselves as a native. Love him as yourself, because you were resident aliens in the land of Egypt.'[22] The reason given (as in Exod. 22.21; 23.9), it should be noted, constitutes an appeal to a kind of common human solidarity: the resident alien deserves consideration because he is in the same position as Israel herself has been in. Indeed the resident alien, because he did not own land, benefits from the same legal provisions as provided a livelihood for the landless Israelite poor (Lev. 19.10; cf. Exod. 22.21—4; Deut. 14.29). Ruth is an example of this principle in operation.

Thus Leviticus 19 itself in principle breaks out of any limitation of love to fellow members of the covenant people. The command to love one's fellow Israelite does not set a limit on love, as though it gave permission not to love anyone else. On the contrary, the extension to include the resident alien suggests that the principle has no limit. It points in the direction of universal love, though the law itself goes no further in this direction. In this sense, Jesus follows the intention of the law when he interprets 'your neighbour', in effect, as 'whoever needs your help' (Luke 10.29–37), and explicitly extends the principle to loving enemies, notably religious enemies (Matt. 5.44–7). The latter is important because love in the Old Testament certainly seems to have had one definite limit: it did not extend to the enemies of God's people, who were God's enemies. The psalmist hates 'with perfect hatred' those who hate God (Ps. 139.21–2). It was in line with this strand of Old Testament thought that some Jews in Jesus' time interpreted Leviticus 19.18b to mean, 'You shall love your neighbour and hate your enemy' (Matt. 5.43). Whether the neighbour is the fellow Jew, or, as in the Qumran community, only the fellow member of the sectarian group which constituted the true Israel, the commandment to love one's neighbour is understood as setting a limit and therefore implying, as its corollary, a command to hate the enemy.[23]

Jesus' rejection of this interpretation is founded, significantly, on God's own love for the wicked (Matt. 5.45). If God loves his enemies, then hatred of Israel's enemies because they are God's enemies cannot be justified. Thus Jesus extends the demand of love, the central principle of the law, into an area where it scarcely penetrated in Old Testament times, though there were occasional forays in that direction, as in the book of Jonah. Israel's relationships to her national enemies must be seen as the area of her national life least touched by the ethical principle at the heart of her law.

3: Wisdom for the Powerful

Proverbs 31: 1—9

Proverbs 31.1—9 (RSV)

1 The words of Lemuel, king of Massa, which his mother taught
  him:
2 What, my son? What, son of my womb?
    What, son of my vows?
3 Give not your strength to women,
    your ways to those who destroy kings.
4 It is not for kings, O Lemuel,
    it is not for kings to drink wine,
    or for rulers to desire strong drink;
5 lest they drink and forget what has been decreed,
    and pervert the rights of all the afflicted.
6 Give strong drink to him who is perishing,
    and wine to those in bitter distress;
7 let them drink and forget their poverty,
    and remember their misery no more.
8 Open your mouth for the dumb,
    for the rights of all who are left desolate.
9 Open your mouth, judge righteously,
    maintain the rights of the poor and needy.

Origin and Old Testament Contexts

This passage of Scripture is doubly unusual, in that its author was
both a woman and a non-Israelite. She was the queen mother of
the Arab kingdom of Massa in north-eastern Arabia (Gen. 25.14).[1]
Perhaps it was because she exercised political authority in her
own right that she undertook what would normally have been the
father's role of instructing a son in the duties of his position in
society.[2] King Lemuel passed on his mother's memorable advice,
in much the same way as the Egyptian Pharaoh Merikare published
his father's rather similar teaching.[3]

41

These facts about the orgin of the passage make it a prime example of the international character of the wisdom material collected in the book of Proverbs. Like Solomon himself (1 Kings 4.29—34), the sages of Israel belonged to a world of international learning. Because their wisdom was not, like the law and the prophets, based on the special salvation history of God's covenant people, but on common human experience, they readily borrowed from foreign wisdom literature. In our passage we have a fully acknowledged borrowing, apparently selected just as it stood for incorporation into the canonical collection of Israel's wisdom. Of course, as part of the whole book of Proverbs, our passage gains a *theological* context (see Prov. 1.7; 2.6) which relates it to the God of Israel, but this is a *creation*-theological context (see especially Prov. 8), not a salvation-historical context. It is therefore a context appropriate to examples of that ethical wisdom which is accessible to human beings as such, as God's creatures in God's world, independently of the special relevatory experience of God's covenant people. That such material became part of the Hebrew canon of Scripture and thus part of the background to God's revelation of himself in Christ is instructive. It shows that there is an important element of continuity between special revelation and general human experience, whatever some theologians may claim to the contrary.

If we bear this in mind as we read the advice of Lemuel's mother, it is instructive, further, to observe that the content of this advice correlates very closely with the concerns of the law and the prophets. Concern for the rights of the weakest members of society, who cannot protect themselves (vv. 8—9), is required of Israel's political and judicial authorities both by the law (e.g. Exod. 23.6) and by the prophets (e.g. Jer. 22.2—3). Lemuel's mother expresses a common ideal of kingship in the ancient Near East, which was also Israel's ideal (Ps. 72.12—14) and became the messianic ideal (Isa. 11.4). The correlation should be encouraging for the Christian engaged in politics today. It is not necessary to assume that the ethical concerns which Christians derive from the Christian revelation will be unrecognizable to non-Christians engaged in politics. If we observe, for example, a genuine convergence between Christian ideals and ideas of human rights formulated on a purely humanistic basis, we do not have to be suspicious, as though this were evidence of Christian accommodation to secular thought. We may well, in fact, have something to learn from secular thought, just as generations of readers of Scripture have learned from Lemuel's mother.

What is lacking from Lemuel's mother's teaching by comparison with corresponding material elsewhere in the Old Testament is the kind of motivation which the latter supplies from the salvation-historical basis of its teaching. For God's own people, concern for the rights of the poor and oppressed follows from their historical experience of God's salvific grace (e.g. Deut. 24.17—18) and from their knowledge of the character of God as he has revealed himself to them (e.g. Deut. 10.17—19; 2 Chron. 19.6—7). But the lack of this redemptive basis does not prevent Lemuel's mother from perceiving the ethical principle at stake—the equal rights of all human beings—and the political principle which follows from that: the special duty of those in power towards those who cannot secure their rights for themselves. The special value of our passage is its memorable expression of this principle.

Lemuel and Merikare

Because Lemuel's mother's advice belongs not only to Israel's scriptures but also to the international wisdom of the time, it is worth comparing it with other manuals of instruction to princes in the ancient Near East. The most comprehensive of these to have survived is the Egyptian work already mentioned: the Instruction for Merikare,[4] which is a treatise on the duties and art of kingship by a Pharaoh whose name has not survived, addressed to his son and heir Merikare.[5] The work has a strong moral and religious tone, exhorting Merikare to rule with justice and beneficence, wisdom and honesty, and appealing to the favour and judgement of the gods as motivation for so doing. The king is to be concerned with the welfare of his subjects and must carefully fulfil his duties towards the religious cult. In the totalitarian despotism of the Pharaohs, the king's duties to his subjects cannot, of course, be separated from his duty to maintain his own power and the integrity of the state, and a good deal of pragmatic advice on these topics is included: how to secure the frontiers, the need to remove potential demagogues and trouble-makers, the duty of punishing rebels much more severely than other criminals, the need to reward officials generously so that they are not corruptible by bribes. In the midst of all these topics, the king's traditional duty to protect the weak also appears, as an important aspect of royal justice: 'Do justice, that you may live long upon earth. Calm the weeper, do not oppress the widow, do not oust a man from his father's property [i.e. do not take advantage of an orphan], do not degrade magnates from their seat' (lines 45–8).[6] It should be noted that the injunction not to use the royal power to the disadvantage of vulnerable groups—the widows and the orphans—is here linked with the injunction not to impoverish the nobility. The overriding concept is the Egyptian hierarchical view of social order: the king should not abuse his position at the summit of the social order to the detriment of his inferiors, but should exercise a superior's responsibilities of justice and beneficence towards his inferiors.[7]

By comparison, the advice of Lemuel's mother is striking, not because its content is unparalleled as such, but because it selects only one theme from the whole range of royal duties. Whereas Merikare's father is concerned to instruct his son in many different facets of kingship, Lemuel's mother directs her remarks solely to the king's overriding duty towards the helpless. Of course, we have no way of knowing whether this selectivity is due to Lemuel's mother herself or to the Hebrew editor who included her teaching in a collection of Israelite wisdom and may have selected only that part of it which interested him. But in either case it is significant that only this aspect of instruction in the duties of kingship has found its way into the book of Proverbs. There is very little advice given specifically to kings elsewhere in the book,[8] and so we must suppose that Lemuel's mother's teaching represents what the wise men of Israel thought really essential in the instruction of a king. They did not think it necessary to mention securing the frontiers, maintaining the cult, or dealing with rebels. They did think it important to stress the king's responsibility to protect the weakest members of society. As we shall see later, this coheres with the general attitude of the Old Testament to kingship.

Detailed Exegesis
The whole passage (Prov. 31.2–9) should be read as a unity, focused on the notion that political power is a responsibility to be exercised for the sake of others, especially those most in need of help and protection, not a privilege to be enjoyed for the king's own advantage. Hence a self-indulgent life must be eschewed, not on grounds of private morality, but as likely to impair the king's exercise of his public responsibilities (vv. 3–5). The function of verses 6–7 is really to reinforce this point by contrast: alcoholic

oblivion is a merciful escape for those in extreme circumstances, who can do nothing to help themselves, but for those who can and should help them it is a flight from responsibility. Simply because of the obvious objections to following the injunctions of verses 6—7 too *literally*, we should not neglect to take them *seriously*: as a compassionate recognition of the extreme misery of the desolate, and as a warning against an over-moralistic attitude to their plight. Lemuel's policy is not to be, 'The king helps those who help themselves,' so much as 'The king helps those who cannot help themselves.'

The context of verses 5, 8—9, is civil and criminal *justice*: note the references to the 'rights' of the underprivileged in all three verses, the reference to laws in verse 5a, and the injunction to 'judge righteously' in verse 9. In biblical societies the great problem of justice was that formal equality before the law, which was enshrined in the law-codes, frequently failed in legal practice, because the process of law was influenced by those with economic and social power. Hence the constant Old Testament concern to protect the weak against corrupt justice (e.g. Deut. 16.19; 2 Chron. 19.7; Amos 5.12). In these circumstances the king as supreme judge had a vital role: he could step in on behalf of those who were being denied their rights in the local courts. Precisely his powerful position enabled him to resist the pressures which prevailed in the local situation and to act as protector of those who had otherwise no protector.[9] It was this role in particular which earned approval for the monarchy in such passages as Psalm 72. But it was a role which required of the king a constant vigilance and a determination not to exploit the advantages of his position.

'Speak out on behalf of the dumb' (v. 8a) need not be metaphorical. Those who were literally dumb were at a clear disadvantage in legal proceedings unless they had someone to speak for them. Not only the rich and powerful, but even the poor could take advantage of them (cf. the injunctions against taking advantage of other kinds of handicapped people in Lev. 19.14). Thus 'the dumb' are an actual instance of the *most* disadvantaged people in society, and as such they stand for all who find it hard to get a hearing for their just rights. Another such category of people is the object of verse 8b (RSV: 'all who are left desolate'), though the precise meaning is uncertain.[10] Some suggested translations indicate another specific class of peculiarly disadvantaged people: 'all who are without understanding', i.e. the mentally subnormal, or 'all children of abandonment', i.e. orphans. Another possibility is the rather more general meaning, 'all victims of circumstances'. Those whose plight is economic are specifically mentioned in verse 9b.

'Open your mouth for the dumb' is the happy phrase which makes this passage especially memorable. It must have been a traditional way of speaking, because we find a comparable statement in Job's account of his exercise of judicial authority (as another non-Israelite chieftain in the same tradition of political ideals): 'I was eyes to the blind, and feet to the lame' (Job 29.15). Similarly also God, as the model of just kingship, is the 'Father of the fatherless and protector of widows' (Ps. 68.5).[11] This way of speaking expresses vividly the king's duty to supply precisely what the disadvantaged person lacks and needs in order to secure his rights. It suggests a kind of solidarity between the powerful and the powerless, in which the person who has political power exercises it on behalf of the powerless. For the Old Testament, it is this kind of exercise of power which justifies the existence of political power. Either the king exercises his power on behalf of the powerless, or else he is the summit of the system of power which oppresses the powerless (cf. 1 Sam. 8.10–18; Eccles. 5.8).

Those New Testament passages which speak in general terms of the judicial functions of the state use more abstract language (Rom. 13.3; 1 Pet. 2.14). But their purpose is to justify the general framework of law and order provided by the Roman Empire, to Christians who might be tempted to rebellion. They are not addressed to rulers, and do not aim to engage with the concrete forms of injustice which the Old Testament's more politically realistic perspective highlights. Thus they do not allow us to blunt the edge of Lemuel's mother's political principle. In a quite different way, as we shall see, the New Testament in fact sharpens that edge.

Interpretation for Today
In very few societies today is there a monarch whose political role corresponds to that of Lemuel, but it is a role which still needs to be played. In many modern societies there are far more developed institutional means of giving the weaker members of society a voice in the political and legislative process and of preventing the corruption of justice. But it remains the case that formal equality before the law cannot in itself prevent laws from operating in the

interests of some and to the unfair disadvantage of others. Nor can the democratic principle of 'one person, one vote' in itself ensure an adequate voice for the disadvantaged minorities of society. Democracy can be the tyranny of the strong majority over the weak minority, and although this may be preferable to the tyranny of a single ruler or a junta, the weakest suffer either way. Not even enlightened self-interest in a democratic system can really replace the moral need for the exercise of power, by all who have a share in political power, on behalf of the powerless.

This requires, in a rapidly changing society, frequent legislative reform. It requires pressure groups. It requires political leaders with real compassion and the courage to look beyond the interests that support them. It requires constant and imaginative vigilance. In our society it is easy for those disadvantaged minorities with articulate spokesmen and a good image to gain a hearing and for those in political power to feel their duties in this respect to be fulfilled by attention to these groups. But the principle of speaking out for the dumb requires continually renewed alertness to the needs of those who are still *dumb*, who cannot speak for themselves, who in some cases may never be able to speak for themselves (the severely mentally handicapped, the very sick, the very old, and children, including the unborn), and who have not yet found those who can speak effectively for them. In a morally healthy democracy political parties and governments should be judged partly by their willingness to take up the cause of such groups, and the responsibility to see that they do is widely diffused among all who have some voice in the political process.

In our world, too, the responsibility to speak out for the dumb is an international one. Amnesty International, Keston College, and various organizations concerned with human rights, including the Churches, are from this point of view essential to the international political process, as are the media, whose power in this respect was so clearly revealed through the case of the Ethiopian famine. Such applications of her principle extend far beyond what the queen mother of Massa could have envisaged herself, but demonstrate its transcultural power.

The Monarchy in Israel

Proverbs 31.1–9 provides an unusual but illuminating point of entry into the question of the Old Testament's attitude to monarchy as a political institution.[12] In many Christian societies of the past, in which monarchical government was taken for granted, appeal was often made to the Israelite monarchy as a model. At its worst this served to justify despotic rule; at its best it infused into the practice of royal government something of the Old Testament ideal of kingship, in which the king's role is to ensure justice for his people. But too often the *ambiguity* of the Old Testament view of the monarchy was neglected. Especially in the doctrine of the divine right of kings, it was forgotten that for Israel monarchy did not, as in the myths of other Near Eastern nations, descend from heaven, but emerged, as a divine concession, from the people's rebellious desire for a king (1 Sam. 8).

In Israel's foundation charter as the covenant people of God—the Pentateuch, which tells the story of her origin and gives her the laws she should live by—the monarchy scarcely features. It appears only in Deuteronomy 17.14—20. This passage, though it makes no explicit criticism of the monarchy, treats it, exactly as 1 Samuel 8 does, as a concession to Israel's own desire to be like the other nations and have a king (Deut. 17.14; cf. 1 Sam. 8.19—20). Moreover, this passage denies the king the customary forms of royal power—many wives, excessive wealth and military forces (Deut. 17.16—17)—and subjects him to the same religious obligations as the rest of the people (Deut. 17.18—19), so that he may not assume despotic power over his 'brothers' and usurp the lordship of God over the people (Deut. 17.20). Kingship is tolerable only if the king remains, so to speak, first among equals.

This passage shows how difficult it was to reconcile monarchy with the fundamental Old Testament conception of Israel as the people of God. It was difficult because Israel originated as a nation of liberated slaves, freed from the tyranny of Egypt, subject only to God their liberator. To wish to be subject to the despotic authority of a king was to despise the freedom God had given them.

Thus monarchy was inconsistent with the early Israelite ideal of a free society of equals under the sole, liberating lordship of God. On these grounds Gideon refused to be king (Judg. 8.23; cf. 1 Sam. 8.7), and the inappropriateness of monarchy in Israel was the lesson also of his son's attempt to be king (Judg. 9). By contrast with the city-states of Canaan, premonarchical Israel was a relatively egalitarian, decentralized, tribal society,[13] over which God maintained his direct rule by raising up charismatic leaders as he chose, rather than sanctioning a dynasty. Such leaders, for all their failings, were much less liable than hereditary monarchs

48

to forget either their solidarity with the people or their responsibility to God. However, we should not idealize the period of the judges: the book of Judges itself certainly does not (see especially Judg. 17.6; 21.25). No doubt there was a degree of historical inevitability about the transition to monarchy, and we should notice that the corrupt role of Samuel's sons as judges (1 Sam. 8.1–5) was the occasion for Israel's desire for a king. At least in part it was for the sake of the justice they expected from a king that the people were prepared to risk the oppression characteristic of ancient monarchies (1 Sam. 8.11–18). Royal justice may often have been, for kings, an ideology to justify their oppression, but for the people it was an ideal they constantly longed to see realized in their rulers.

The rise of the dynastic monarchy accompanied large-scale changes in Israelite society: centralized government, bureaucracy, the partial replacement of the clan system by a class system, the growth of economic inequalities. The social and economic injustices denounced by the prophets were the products of these changes. In relation to the monarchy, however, the strategy of the prophets was not to declare it illegitimate so much as to judge it by the standard of the ideal which alone could justify it. Monarchy could be justified at all only if it served, instead of usurping and frustrating, God's own liberating rule over his people. It could do so principally by executing justice for the victims of oppression: this is the ideal of kingship which the prophets set critically against the actual practice of kingship in Israel (cf. Jer. 21.12; 22.3, 15–16; Ezek. 34.4).

Thus the monarchy, denounced, by and large, for its actual practice, could be rescued as a critical ideal by putting it at the service of one of Israel's original political aims: God's liberating justice for the oppressed. It could be understood in this way because the king's responsibility to ensure justice for the most vulnerable members of society was already, in any case, part of the common Near Eastern concept of kingship, which Israel took over when she accepted a king in order to be 'like all the nations' (1 Sam. 8.20). In this way we can see how Proverbs 31.1–9 coheres with the whole thrust of the Old Testament's thinking about the monarchy. It selects and stresses—as what kingship is really all about—precisely that aspect of the royal duties, as understood in international wisdom, which alone could make monarchy relatively acceptable to those, like the prophets, who stood for God's rule over his people and his concern for justice. It leaves aside all the more questionable aspects of monarchy—military might, centralized bureaucratic control, hierarchical ideology and economic inequality—of which other strands of Old Testament thought are critical, and focuses exclusively on the king's exercise of power for protecting the rights of the powerless.

Thus in view of the fundamental resistance to despotism in Israel's religious traditions, the Old Testament can give unqualified approval only to an idealized version of the monarchy. The coronation psalm, Psalm 72, is most instructive here. It prays that the king may execute justice and reign prosperously, and the thorough interweaving of the two themes shows that the prosperity is dependent on the justice. The justice he is to exercise is *God's* (v. 1), and so it is justice for the poor and needy, deliverance for the oppressed, support for the weak who have no one else to help them (vv. 2, 4, 12—14). If the king is the Lord's anointed, if God sanctions his rule, this is only because and in so far as his rule reflects God's. In view of the almost constant disappointment of this expectation, the *hope* for a king who would fulfil the ideal arose. In the messianic expectation kingship has nothing to do with domination and oppression, but solely with God's liberating lordship (cf. Isa. 9.7; 11.3—4; Jer. 23.5; 33.15). Like the Deuteronomic ideal, the messianic king will rule in solidarity with his brothers because, like the ideal king of Psalm 72, he implements God's concern for the vulnerable and the neglected.

The Old Testament cannot be understood to prescribe a particular political system for later societies. What it does provide is a criterion for assessing all political systems and their practice: that government must be exercised on behalf of all the people, in the interests of all, and especially in the interests of those who would otherwise suffer most, the weakest and most disadvantaged, those without any social or economic power or influence. It may well be that some political systems are more likely to fulfil this aim than others. At any rate, under most modern conditions, some form of democracy seems much more likely than monarchy to do so. But the system must be kept subordinate to the aim. Since no system can *guarantee* the fulfilment of the aim, the aim needs to be constantly reasserted and secured in an endless variety of ways, as we have already seen.

A Christological Reflection
As we have seen, it was the same ideal of kingship as is expressed

in Proverbs 31.1—9 which formed the Jewish messianic expectation and so provided that political aspect of Messiahship which Jesus did not so much reject as radicalize, in a way which took it beyond the reach of human politics. The Messiah exercises his kingship not as a privilege to be exploited, but in the service of all (Luke 22.24—7): this is in the tradition of Lemuel's mother's advice. But this king's solidarity with the powerless takes the form of radical identification with them in their helpless circumstances: here he follows the tradition beyond itself.

Surprisingly at first—but only at first—it is with verses 6—7 of our passage that the story of Jesus makes explicit connection. Evidently in obedience to Proverbs 31.6, the women of Jerusalem were accustomed to offering wine, mingled with myrrh to increase its narcotic effect, to those condemned to execution.[14] Jesus, offered such a drink on the way to crucifixion (Mark 15.23), was thus identified with those most wretched members of society whose misery is unbearable. At the same time, in refusing the drink, Jesus showed himself to be not just one of them, another helpless victim of circumstances, but one who voluntarily undertook to share their sufferings and in full consciousness bear for them what for them was unbearable. Thus he is the king who, in radical solidarity with the helpless (Prov. 31.6—7) himself eschews wine out of his responsibility for the helpless (Prov. 31.4—5). The solidarity of the powerful with the powerless becomes in him the power of solidarity in powerlessness—or, in Paul's terms, the power of God's weakness (1 Cor. 1.25).

That Jesus' living out of ideal (messianic) kingship took the form of this extreme solidarity with the wretched is in several ways a challenge to our thinking about the exercise of political power. In the first place, it contests the authority of any political power which, like Caiaphas and Pilate, prefers expediency to justice and compassion. The king of kings did not sit in judgement with Caiaphas and Pilate, but suffered their condemnation and in doing so condemned them.

Second, Jesus' radical solidarity with the helpless is an impossible ideal for the politicians, but nevertheless one which they may not neglect. In politics the solidarity of the powerful with the powerless is effective on their behalf because the powerful remain powerful and exercise their power on behalf of the powerless. But political power can easily distance its holders from the powerless. They do not really know what it is like to be powerless, or, even if they once knew, they forget (cf. Eccles. 4.13−14). They may claim to speak for the powerless, but the powerless do not feel them to be their spokespersons. At worst, the powerless become pawns in the political power-game played by their professed spokespersons, and are all the more useful because they have no voice of their own to protest. Here Jesus' example can remind even politicians what solidarity really demands. Politicians may not, in normal circumstances, renounce power, but they must resist its distancing effect in whatever ways are open to them.

Finally, however, Jesus' solidarity with the helpless reminds us of the limitations of politics, important though politics is. There are ways of following Jesus in loving solidarity with the most disadvantaged people which go beyond the scope of political solutions to their problems. The political authorities can, for example, aid Mother Teresa's work, but they cannot do it.

4: Songs for the Oppressed

Psalms 10 and 126

Though the Old Testament often speaks in favour of the oppressed, it is not always the oppressed themselves who speak in it. Some of the psalms, however, are the voice of the oppressed. From them we can learn something about *prayer* and politics in situations where faith is both tested and inspired. This chapter will make considerable use of the writings of modern Christians in situations of political oppression, since when it comes to understanding the biblical prayers of the oppressed, those who turn to God in circumstances of oppression today have a hermeneutical privilege.

Psalm 10 (RSV)

1   Why dost thou stand afar off, O LORD?
      Why dost thou hide thyself in times of trouble?
2   In arrogance the wicked hotly pursue the poor;
      let them be caught in the schemes which they have devised.

3   For the wicked boasts of the desires of his heart,
      and the man greedy for gain curses and renounces the LORD.
4   In the pride of his countenance the wicked does not seek him;
      and all his thoughts are, 'There is no God.'

5   His ways prosper at all times;
      thy judgments are on high, out of his sight;
      as for all his foes, he puffs at them.
6   He thinks in his heart, 'I shall not be moved;
      throughout all generations I shall not meet adversity.'

7   His mouth is filled with cursing and deceit and oppression;
      under his tongue are mischief and iniquity.
8   He sits in ambush in the villages;
      in hiding places he murders the innocent.

9   His eyes stealthily watch for the hapless,
      he lurks in secret like a lion in his covert;

he lurks that he may seize the poor,
    he seizes the poor when he draws him into his net.

10 The hapless is crushed, sinks down,
      and falls by his might.
11 He thinks in his heart, 'God has forgotten,
      he has hidden his face, he will never see it.'

12 Arise, O LORD; O God, lift up thy hand;
      forget not the afflicted.
13 Why does the wicked renounce God,
      and say in his heart, 'Thou wilt not call to account'?

14 Thou dost see; yea, thou dost note trouble and vexation,
      that thou mayst take it into thy hands;
    the hapless commits himself to thee;
      thou hast been the helper of the fatherless.

15 Break thou the arm of the wicked and evildoer;
      seek out his wickedness till thou find none.
16 The LORD is king for ever and ever;
      the nations shall perish from his land.

17 O LORD, thou wilt hear the desire of the meek;
      thou wilt strengthen their heart, thou wilt incline thy ear
18 to do justice to the fatherless and the oppressed,
      so that man who is of the earth may strike terror no more.

A Cry from the Depths

Psalm 10[1] is one of the so-called psalms of lament, which would
be better called psalms of complaint or protest.[2] They are cries
from the depths by people who cannot bear their suffering any
longer. Far from resigning themselves to it—as the term 'lament'
might suggest—they protest against it, often indignantly, bitterly,
with desperation. They complain to God, but often in terms which
amount to a complaint *against* God, who has left them to suffer.
'Why, O Lord?' and 'How long, O Lord?' are the anguished
questions which characterize these prayers.

Besides the psalmist and his God, there is always also a third
party: the psalmist's enemies. These may lurk in the background,
but frequently they move threateningly into the foreground of the
picture the psalmist paints. Even if his suffering seems initially to
have other causes—such as illness—there are always enemies

quick to gloat, to mock, and to take advantage of his weakness. The context of *social conflict* is inescapable in these psalms. It produces the feature of them which many modern readers find objectionable: the psalmist's desire for vengeance on his enemies. Such readers often have an even more fundamental lack of sympathy with these psalms, because, living in peaceful and affluent conditions, they scarcely know what it is to have enemies in the sense the psalmist had. Such people, if they see the petty animosities and conflicts of their own lives for what they are, find the psalmist's constant preoccupation with his enemies strange. So it is as well to begin by recognizing the situation of social conflict behind these psalms. The psalmists' desperation derives from social and economic weakness. Either they are the victims of oppression by the rich and powerful, or they find that, if for one reason or another they are down on their luck, even their ordinary neighbours, people they had counted their friends, now shun them or actively take advantage.

In Psalm 10 the situation of social injustice is obvious and central to the complaint. Moreover, here the psalmist complains not only on his own behalf and seeks justice not only for himself, but for a whole class of 'poor' people who are oppressed by 'the wicked'. The wicked are people who pursue profit (v. 3) to the exclusion of all other considerations. The images—standard in the psalms—of the wicked man as a wild animal, lying in wait to seize the poor (v. 10), and a hunter, who traps the poor in his net (v. 11), emphasize the vulnerability of the poor, who are powerless and without protection against the exploitation and violence of the powerful. The 'poor' or 'afflicted' (vv. 2, 9, 12) are also described as 'oppressed' or 'exploited' (v. 18), and, significantly, as orphans (vv. 14, 18). This does not mean that the psalmist is literally an orphan, but that he puts himself in that class of people who were characteristically represented by the orphan: those whose social and economic position was weakest, the most vulnerable and defenceless, those who have no one to protect their rights. No one, that is, except God, who is 'the helper of orphans' (v. 14). Some commentators stress that in the psalms the term 'poor' has become a religious, more than an economic, term, for those who adopt an attitude of humility and dependence in relation to God.[3] In psalm 10—and probably most others—it is patently not the case that a religious meaning has replaced the social and economic. But it is true that the social and economic plight of the psalmist has a direct religious implication: having no other resource, he is wholly dependent on God for protection and justice. For the God of Israel is peculiarly the helper of the helpless: it is his characteristic role to step in on behalf of the oppressed and the downtrodden.

But so far he has not done so: this is the psalmist's cause for complaint: 'Why do you stand far off, O Lord: why do you hide your face in time of need?' (v. 1, LP). The psalms of complaint characteristically move from complaint through petition to assurance of being heard by God. Here the complaint moves from the 'Why?' of v. 1 to the 'Why?' of v. 13; petition breaks in in v. 12 and gains assurance in vv. 14–15; the psalm concludes with the confidence that God has heard and will respond (vv. 16–18). Thus complaint is not the last word in this psalm (as it is in just one psalm, the darkest in the psalter, Psalm 88). But it is given full scope for expression. The psalmists never restrain their language or censor their feelings. It is essential to their relationship with God that they do not. In the situation of abandonment by God, it is only in the full expression of bitterness and protest that they maintain their dialogue with God and so win through to confidence and hope.

Thus it is important to listen attentively to the psalmist's complaint and not hurry on too quickly to its resolution. We have to enter his darkness. For those who are already there with him in the depths, his words are an aid to expressing their own complaint and to discovering that even in God's absence he can still be addressed. For those who are not in a comparable situation, the psalm brings to our attention the darkness that really exists in the world and forbids us to cover it over with easy religious comfort. It draws us into solidarity with those victimized people who can only cry out in protest to a God whose face is hidden from them.

Why, Lord?

The cogency of the psalmist's complaint depends on the connection he makes between God and social justice. In the absence of social justice (vv. 2–11) he perceives the absence of God (v. 1). Moreover, *so do the wicked*. The wicked man is portrayed as a practical atheist: '"There is no God" is all his thought' (v. 4, LP). This does not mean that he makes a formal denial of the existence of God, which was scarcely an intellectual possibility at the time, but that he leaves God entirely out of account in his behaviour. He acts on the premise that God is not interested in social justice and

will take no action to ensure it. The 'arrogance' of the wicked is his
open defiance of morality, his confidence that he can exploit the
poor with impunity (vv. 2a, 3—4, 6). As he crushes the weak, 'he
thinks in his heart, "God has forgotten, he has hidden his face, he
will never see it"' (v. 11, RSV). But this is exactly the substance of
the psalmist's own complaint (v. 1): that God hides his face,
ignores flagrant injustice, does not call the wicked to account. It
looks as though the wicked are correct! It looks as though the
world is in fact such that exploitation of the poor is the key to
success (vv. 5—6). We glimpse the depths from which the
psalmist's complaint arises only when we see the threat, implicit
in the situation, that the practical atheism of the wicked could
prove to be true. The psalmist's complaint is that, for all practical
purposes, 'there is no God'—no God such as Israel has believed in,
no God of the Exodus, no God who sees injustice, cares for the
oppressed, and intervenes on their behalf. Hence the first why?
question (v. 1: 'Why do you hide your face in time of need?') is in
substance the same as the second why? question: 'Why should the
wicked man spurn God: why should he say in his heart, "He will
not avenge"?' (v. 13, LP).

The complaint is thus a version of the *theodicy* question: Why
does God allow evil? How can God be God if he does so? Three
aspects of the question as it is posed in this psalm are worth
noting. First, it is characteristic of ancient Israel that the question
arises in the context of *social* evil.[4] It is not a speculative question
for armchair philosophy, but a life-and-death question of
marginalized people in the struggle to survive. But, second, it is
also characteristic of Old Testament faith that the question is put
to God. There is a paradox in the psalmist's complaint *to God* that
God hides his face and does not see, because the complaint is itself
an act of faith that God does see and so can be addressed. The
tension in this paradox is very considerable, but it saves the
psalmist from the deadly despair which would follow from yielding
to the threat that the practical atheism of the wicked is true. A
God who can be addressed, to whom can be addressed even the
complaint that he is deaf, constitutes the only hope that injustice
will not have the final say in life. Faith in this God, in the face of
contradiction, *matters* in a way which makes the easy agnosticism
of the modern West seem trivial. 'For the victims, belief in God is
not an intellectual exercise, but the presence or absence of hope.'[5]

Third, the psalmist's question, 'Why?', demands an active, not a theoretical response. It does not really want an *explanation* of God's apparent absence, so much as an end to it. Concretely, it requires justice for the oppressed (v. 18) and retribution for the oppressors (v. 2b).

The theodicy question inevitably arises in situations of political evil and oppression. Carl Friedrich Goerdeler, the mayor of Leipzig whose Christian convictions drove him into the German resistance to Hitler, wrote from prison in 1945, after being sentenced to death:

> Is there a God who takes part in the personal destiny of man? It becomes difficult for me to believe so, for this God has now for years permitted torrents of blood and suffering, mountains of horror and despair, to be engendered against mankind by a few hundred thousand bestialised, spiritually diseased, and deluded individuals . . . He has allowed millions of decent people to suffer and die.[6]

Pursuing the question, Goerdeler stumbles upon an *explanation*, of a sort, in the evil of Nazi nationalism:

> Is it not possible that with our arbitrary nationalism we have affronted God and practised idolatry? Yes, in that case the things that are happening would have meaning: God desires to root out thoroughly in all nations the propensity to harness him to their national ambitions. If this be true, we can only beg God to let it suffice, and in the place of tears and death, to give ascendancy to the apostles of reconciliation who have recognised this spirit in God and this purpose in his judgments. For this I pray to him.[7]

Had it been offered from the remote security of an academic study, the explanation of God's purpose in such suffering would be dubious. It gains authenticity from its speaker in his context, as one who shared and worked to end the suffering. And observing the post-Nazi world, we can see some validity in it. But the Nazi horror still exceeds any such explanation. Attempts to understand God's purpose in political evils have a certain validity, but their questions, like Job's, are often unanswered. Above all, they lose all validity if their theoretical explanations sap the force of the biblical theodicy question in its drive towards an active response: the removal of injustice and an end to the suffering. For those who suffer injustice, God remains God only as he remains the hope for justice. Thus Goerdeler's response to the theodicy question is an authentic one in that, not content with explanation, he presses on, with the psalmist, to petition: 'If this be true, we can only beg God to let it suffice . . .'

'You strengthen the hearts of the afflicted'
As he moves from complaint to petition, the psalmist discovers that the God who can still be addressed is the God who still hears, and thereby he attains to confidence and hope. On the one hand, this discovery is possible only through the full expression of his complaint to God, but, on the other hand, it is not some devotional achievement of his own: it breaks into his darkness as the grace of God surprisingly present in suffering. The abrupt assurance of verse 14, contradicting the self-confidence of the wicked in verse 13, is *given*: 'You have seen the trouble and vexation, yes you have!'[8]

God is not absent if he hears, and if he hears he will not fail to act. For the God on whom the psalmist finds himself able, after all, to rely, is the one whom Israel has known since the Exodus to be the God who *responds* in deliverance to the cry of the helpless (v. 14b). The theology of the psalms of complaint is essentially the Exodus theology: 'Then we cried to the LORD the God of our fathers, and the LORD heard our voice, and saw our affliction, our toil, and our oppression; and the LORD brought us out of Egypt with a mighty hand . . .' (Deut. 26.7−8; cf. Exod. 3.7−8). The sequence is the same: the oppressed complain, God hears, God delivers.[9] This is the point of the triumphant affirmation of God's kingship in Psalm 10.16: 'The LORD is king for ever and ever.' It echoes the triumphant conclusion to the song of Israel at the Red Sea: 'The LORD will reign for ever and ever' (Exod. 15.18). God's kingship is not his sanction for unjust earthly power−neither Pharaoh's nor the psalmist's oppressors'. Rather it is the court of appeal for those who cannot get justice from earthly powers. If God is king, then unjust social and political conditions must be open to change. God, who does, of course, sanction just political and social order, is the power for transformation of unjust order, on behalf of the weak and the powerless. Therefore, against the arrogant self-reliance of the wicked, who suppose that nothing will ever shake their affluent security (v. 6), the psalmist relies on the truly unshakeable, eternal rule of God (v. 16). 'For Israel what is found at the bottom of the pit is not *despair* but *the rule of God.*

Israel knows that the rule of God is the only alternative to despair.'[10]

When the psalm is written, the psalmist confidently anticipates deliverance, but it has not yet happened. It would be naive for us to suppose that he could not have had long to wait. God's grace is not manipulatable by our prayer. But his new confidence and hope in God have *already* transformed the psalmist's situation. In the knowledge that God is not absent, but with him, he has a new inner strength to resist the destructive effects of his situation. His enemies cannot crush his spirit or extinguish his thirst for justice. Not that this inner liberation, as we might call it, is any substitute for actual social change: it is no opium for the people. Rather it sustains the spirit of resistance to injustice in hope of justice:

Yahweh, you listen to the wants of the humble,
you bring strength to their hearts, you grant them a hearing,
judging in favour of the orphaned and exploited,
so that earthborn man may strike fear no longer (vv. 17—18, JB).

Authentic prayer in the midst of oppression that continues without realistic sight of an end is no doubt the most difficult and at the same time the most necessary form of political prayer. God is at once the source of impatience for justice and freedom, rage against injustice, perplexity at its continuance, comfort in extremity, strength to continue hoping. The South African poet Walter M. B. Nhlapo writes:[11]

Rising in the morn I cry,
'Come Freedom today!'
At midday I sit and sigh,
'When comes the great day?'

God! To Thee I bring my sorrow,
Tears I daily weep;
Must they be my food tomorrow?
If so, give me sleep!

In such circumstances, the breakthrough of the psalmists from complaint to hope must be a continual experience. The one constant factor is that God is the one who can always be addressed, even in his absence, and, in being addressed, is found to be near.

A Psalm from Namibia

The following prayer, which I call a psalm because it reflects the spirit, as well as sometimes the words, of the biblical psalms of complaint, was written in 1976 by Pastor Zephania Kameeta of the Evangelical Lutheran Church in Namibia. The date explains the topical references. The Soweto uprising and its bloody suppression had happened only ten weeks before. In Namibia, the Turnhalle constitutional conference, convened by the South African government to find a new constitutional arrangement acceptable to their interests in the country, was in session. The SWAPO leader Herman Toivo ya Toivo had already served eight years imprisonment on Robben Island, along with Nelson Mandela. Aaron Mushimba, also a SWAPO leader, was, at the time of writing, under sentence of death, though his conviction was later set aside on appeal. The militarization of northern Namibia, in the intensification of the war against SWAPO forces based in southern Angola, was under way. The diamond mines at Oranjemund and the uranium mine at Rössing are prime examples of Namibia's mineral wealth, for the sake of which the Namibian people have been dominated and exploited, and which explains the South African government's stubborn determination to keep Namibia under the economic control of white South Africa. By these topical references the protest, the petition and the hope of the biblical psalms of complaint find contemporary re-expression in a concrete situation of continuing modern political oppression.

Why, O why, Lord

You know, Lord, what is going on, this moment,
in the hearts of Toivo ya Toivo,
Nelson Mandela and Aaron Mushimba.
Certainly you know the hearts of my brethren
their daily sufferings, far away on the vast
and lonely weald, among the sheep.
You see them despised and neglected,
paid a mere trifle; you read their thoughts
deep down in the pits, where they are slaving
for next to nothing.

Lord, the many new graves of the children from Soweto
are well known to you, and so are the tears

61

of their parents and comrades. You are undeceived
by the reasoning and hypocrisy of Turnhalle;
you have observed the hundreds of prisoners
maltreated in the camps of north Namibia.
They are cruelly struck with the butt-ends of rifles;
cigarettes are put out against their naked bodies.
We are miserable and afflicted like the children
of Israel in Egypt. And you are aware of it all.

Why, O why, Lord?
Why do you seem deaf to our doleful cries?
Or have you turned your back upon us?
How long will you allow them to trample us underfoot?
Is our trust nothing to you, is our hope in vain?
Why, why, why do you keep us waiting?

Why, O why, Lord?
Why did you create us? Did you make us only to be shot
like dogs infected with rabies? Did you make us to be
oppressed and put to scorn for ever? Why, Lord, why?
Are there limits to your love, and are we expelled?
Did you make us 'Kaffers,' 'Bantus,' 'Non-whites'?

Were we doomed to stand humbly at the back door of the 'Baas,'
receiving a splash of water from a rusty marmalade tin?
Did you create us to live on 'Yea, Baas' and 'Yea, Missus'?
Did you make us the human caricatures of this world?
Why, O why, Lord, did you create us?

Why, O why, Lord?
Why did you tell us through your word that we were made
in your own image? Why this teaching that, regardless of language,
race and colour, all men are equal in your eyes,
and that we ought to treat and accept each other as such?
Why did you make us realize that our slavery is at an end,
that we are liberated men and women, bought at a high price
with the blood of your only Son? It might have been better
if you had let us alone in our blindness; it would have been
easier then to submit to our fate. It is impossible now.
We have been brought to see, for ourselves,
that we are incomparably more precious than all diamonds
from Oranjemund and all uranium from Rössing.
Why, O why, Lord, did you open our eyes?

Why, O why, Lord?
Why don't you answer when we cry out to you? How long
will you remain passive, looking silently at our agony
and our tears? The yoke has become unendurable,
we won't carry it one step farther.
Why do you allow iniquity and lies to rule over us,
you who redeemed us at the cost of your own life?
You are King of kings and they struck you with their
fists and cudgels; they spat upon you to show their
utter contempt! Cruel nails pierced your hands and feet,
and all this only because of your great and infinite
love for us. Why, O why then are you silent?

From the depths we call to you: Save us in our distress!
Guide us in the right way to Namibia, and not
to a neo-colonial Southwest Africa.
O Lord of the whole world,
refresh our souls and make them new; we are consumed
with thirst for release, righteousness, redemption,
Shalom. Fill our callous, empty hands with your good gifts.
Crush the copper gates and shatter the iron locks
of Robben Island. Break up the prison camps where
our brethren are captive and tortured, help them, Lord!
We call to you, save us in our deadly fear!
We are trembling and feeble. Take our destiny in your
strong right hand; through us let the world see your wonders!
Give us the Spirit of Life so that we may arise.
Then help us to raise, unwearyingly, under your guidance,
the beacons of your kingdom in this country! Amen.[12]

Forsaken in the Desert

Not only the oppressed experience the absence of God. Bishop
Helder Camara writes of 'the inevitable desert' into which those
who work for justice for the oppressed find themselves led:

> If we are to be pilgrims for justice and peace, we must expect the
> desert.
>   The great and the powerful disappear, stop helping us and
> turn against us. They finance campaigns which become shriller
> with lies the closer they feel the danger coming. And what is
> worse, those who are not powerful also avoid us. They are

frightened. Someone who depends entirely on the boss for housing, work and livelihood, is afraid of losing them for himself and especially his family. His natural and understandable reaction is to run away. There are others who are less dependent on the rich, or more aware of the situation, who are ready for anything.

Those are times when we look about us and feel we are an awkward friend. People who welcome us are suspect. They want our friendship but they are afraid of being compromised by our reputation.

We feel we are speaking in a desert, as did all those who were active in the cause of justice before us. Injustice spreads and becomes worse. It has two thirds of the earth in its grip. Only the stones listen. Or men with hearts of stone.

Our weariness spreads from the body to the soul. Which is worse than any bodily exhaustion.

We feel the desert round us as far as our eyes can see. Soft sand which we sink in up to our knees. Blinding and burning sand storms, which hurt our face, get in our eyes and ears . . .

We reach the limit of endurance, desert all about us, desert within. We feel that the Father himself has abandoned us. 'Why hast thou forsaken me?' . . .

We must not trust in our own strength, we must not give way to bitterness, we must stay humble knowing that we are in the hands of God, we must want only to share in the making of a better world. Then we shall not lose our courage or our hope. We shall feel the invisible protection of God our Father.[13]

In the last two paragraphs there is the psalmist's movement from forsakenness and complaint to confidence and hope. It is no coincidence that Camara expresses the experience of forsakenness in the opening words of a psalm of complaint (Ps. 22) which Jesus prayed on the cross (Mark 15.34).

The Psalmists' Prayers and Jesus' Prayers

In his cry from the cross, 'My God, my God, why have you forsaken me?', Jesus identified with the situation and the protest of the psalmists and all who had prayed the psalms of complaint. He entered their darkness. This was well understood by the early Church: the gospel narratives of Gethsemane and the crucifixion are full of quotations from and allusions to the psalms of complaint.[14] In the early Church's reading of these psalms as prophetic of Jesus the deepest meaning is that Jesus voluntarily (as Gethsemane makes clear) identified with all whose affliction finds a voice in such psalms. The political dimension of this by no means exhausts its meaning, but nor should it be suppressed. Jesus, who took up the cause of the poor and oppressed, died a victim of political injustice. He was defenceless against the power of enemies, whose taunts the evangelist puts into words the psalmist had attributed to *his* enemies (Matt. 27.43; Ps. 22.8).

The psalmist, in the darkness of God's absence, found God there with him in the darkness, and the darkness already 'strangely transformed . . . by the power of relentless solidarity'.[15] In entering the psalmist's darkness and taking up the psalmist's protest Jesus became that solidarity of God with all who experience God's absence. Bishop Hanns Lilje, who experienced God as never before in the darkness of a Nazi prison cell, recalled the night of an air raid, when the prison warders had disappeared into the air-raid shelters, leaving the prisoners in their cells. Lilje was visited in his cell by another prisoner, Freiherr von Guttenberg, who, on such occasions, managed at great risk to himself to bring comfort to other prisoners. They talked about Jesus in Gethsemane:

> I shall never forget . . . this whispered conversation about the Son of God, who on that night on the Mount of Olives lifted the horror from every other human night; henceforth He is for ever with those who suffer and struggle and pray in the darkness. Nor shall I ever forget this man: he was one of those who was never so absorbed in his own fate that he forgot the fate of his people.[16]

This was human solidarity rooted in the divine solidarity.

The oppressed Christian who discovers Jesus' solidarity with him must take account of one respect in which Jesus in his suffering prayed differently from the way the psalmists prayed. Jesus prayed for his enemies' forgiveness (Luke 23.34), thus practising his own teaching (Matt. 5.44). The psalmists never did this: their attitude to their enemies is consistently unforgiving. They pray for God's judgement on their enemies (Ps. 10.2b, 15), sometimes in the form of solemn and extensive curses (Ps. 69. 22−8; 109.6−20). But such prayers are not unknown in the New Testament (Rev. 6.10). They need to be accorded a kind of provisional validity, which does not excuse any Christian from the duty of forgiving enemies but does help us to understand what is really involved in forgiveness. Jesus' demand for forgiveness of enemies does not, we might say, simply revoke these prayers, but takes a step further beyond them. We have to appreciate what is valid about them before we can rightly take, as followers of Jesus must take, that further step.

First, these prayers spring directly from the psalmists' demand for justice. Like the widow in Jesus' parable, whose demand was for the judge to vindicate her against her adversary (Luke 18.3), the psalmists' *primary* concern is positive—justice *for* the oppressed—but they cannot envisage this without its negative corollary—justice *against* the oppressor. Nor, in concrete situations of political injustice, is it often easy for us to do otherwise. Our prayers in and about such situations are not superior but inferior to the psalms if they do not manifest the psalmists' thirst for justice and anger at injustice. As John Goldingay writes, 'If we do not find ourselves wishing to call down a curse of divine magnitude on some perpetrators of evil, this may reflect our spiritual sensitivity, our good fortune in not being confronted by evil of such measure, or it may reflect our moral indifference.'[17] Love and forgiveness of enemies should not be invoked to sanction an easy and careless disregard for justice. The force of Jesus' command to love enemies is lost if we forget that it presupposes real *enemies* and makes no attempt to pretend that they are not enemies. Love and forgiveness of enemies are authentic only as the costly and difficult step beyond the psalmists' valid demand for justice.

Second, the psalmists' *prayer* for justice serves *in principle* to protect their concern for justice from degenerating into vindictiveness, even if it does not always do this in practice. The prayer is essentially for God to execute justice, and draws the psalmist, beyond feelings of personal vindictiveness, into a desire to see God's justice prevail. Admittedly, it is possible for talk of divine justice to be used in the interests of personal revenge. But the believer who is genuinely open to God in prayer is subordinating his own judgement of the situation to the standard of God's righteous judgement. The psalms can be used by Christians in this spirit, and most safely with stress (as their hermeneutical key) on such verses as those to which Dietrich Bonhoeffer referred in 1944 as expressions of his hope for God's action in Nazi Germany:

'Surely there is a God who judges on earth' (Ps. 58.11b, RSV), and

> Arise, O LORD! Let not man prevail;
> let the nations be judged before thee!
> Put them in fear, O LORD!
> Let the nations know that they are but men! (Ps. 9.19—20)[18]

Third, the referring of the situation to *God's* justice is the first step towards love and forgiveness of enemies. In expressing to God their rage against their oppressors and their desire for vengeance the psalmists are at least submitting and yielding those wishes to God, even *relinquishing* them to God.[19] Personal vengeance can be renounced, because one's cause has been entrusted to the just God who claims vengeance as his own concern (Deut. 32.35—6; Rom. 12.19). Hanns Lilje provides again a notable example of this in practice. His trial by the Nazis was a travesty of justice which provoked him to furious resentment, against, in particular, the notorious judge Freisler:

> It was the only moment in my whole imprisonment when my blood boiled, and I felt a dark surge of hatred rising up from the very depths of my being. As we travelled back to the prison, all I could do to control my feelings was to make a definite and repeated act of literal obedience to a sentence from the Bible: 'Vengeance is Mine. I will repay, saith the Lord' [Rom. 12.19, citing Deut. 32.35]. I did this with the simplicity of a child. I certainly had plenty of occasion to repeat it over and over again.[20]

It is with reference to such situations that we can appreciate Paul's advice in Romans 12.19. In the course of repeating Jesus' demand for love of enemies—blessing, not cursing them (v. 14), not retaliating (v. 17)—he forbids his readers to avenge themselves (v. 19a), but does not require them to renounce their concern for justice. Rather this can be left in God's hands (v. 19b). *This* then frees them to treat their enemies forgivingly and to welcome their repentance (v. 20). Where those in the grip of personal vengeance must be frustrated, like Jonah, when repentant enemies are spared judgement, those who have committed vengeance to God can promote and rejoice in the compassion by which he at once safeguards and surpasses justice. They can pray for their enemies' forgiveness.

Thus the psalmists' prayers *against* their enemies have a provisional validity. But the disciples of Jesus are nevertheless required and enabled to pray forgivingly *for* their enemies. Such forgiveness is wholly relevant to politics. A liberation struggle which takes its stand on justice but knows nothing of forgiveness becomes all too easily the mirror-image of the oppressive regime it opposes. It returns hatred for hatred. Justice becomes a term for the exclusive interests of the oppressed and other people become dispensable. This is hard to criticize while the oppressed are the oppressed, but its result is that, with 'liberation', the oppressed, or some of them, become new oppressors. Not that justice can be set aside in a spurious kind of reconciliation that changes nothing. But if reconciliation is ever to occur, if a destructive spiral of hatred is to be avoided, desire for justice must go hand in hand with a spirit of forgiveness all along.

Jesus' prayer, 'Father, forgive them; *for they know not what they do*' (Luke 23.34), makes the very difficult demand of loving *understanding* of enemies. In oppressive societies it requires the attempt to understand the structures of sin and ideology in which people of the dominant class are caught and which help to explain why those people feel and think and act as they do—to understand, for example, that the average white South African is no more (and no less) *personally* wicked than most people, but is systematically blinded to the evil he or she helps to perpetrate. Not that to understand everything is to excuse everything. But love for enemies finds possibilities for change and reconciliation which mere desire for justice, however justified in itself, would never discover. Such possibilities open up when love dreams of a different future.

We Have a Dream
Celebrated words from Martin Luther King's speech in Washington, DC, in 1963:

> I have a dream that one day on the red hills of Georgia, sons of former slaves and sons of former slave-owners will be able to sit down together at the table of brotherhood.
>
> I have a dream that one day, even the state of Mississippi, a state sweltering with the heat of injustice, sweltering with the heat of oppression, will be transformed into an oasis of freedom and justice.
>
> I have a dream my four little children will one day live in a

nation where they will not be judged by the color of their skin but by the content of their character. I have a dream today!

I have a dream that one day, down in Alabama, with its vicious racists, with its governor having his lips dripping with the words of interposition and nullification, that one day, right there in Alabama, little black boys and black girls will be able to join hands with little white boys and white girls as sisters and brothers. I have a dream today!

I have a dream that one day every valley will be exalted, every hill and mountain shall be made low, the rough places shall be made plain, and the crooked places shall be made straight and the glory of the Lord will be revealed and all flesh shall see it together.[21]

It is in this sense of 'dream'—a prophetic dream of an inviting future of freedom and justice which contrasts with the evils of the present—that the people of Israel in Psalm 126 compare themselves with dreamers:[22]

Psalm 126.1—3[23]

1 When the LORD restored the fortunes of Zion
   —we are like those who dream—
2 then our mouth was filled with laughter,
   and our tongue with shouts of joy;
   then they said among the nations,
   'The LORD has done great things for them.'
3 The LORD has done great things for us;
   we are glad.

As often in the Old Testament, dreaming is here the vehicle of prophetic vision, though by *comparing* themselves with those who dream the community may be claiming something less than actual prophetic revelation. But with eager, expectant hope, *like* that of the visionary, they anticipate the time when God will reverse their present plight—probably the desolation following the Babylonian destruction of Jerusalem.[24] They anticipate it with a vividness comparable with Martin Luther King's, so that it seems already present to them, their mouths already fill with laughter, the actual sorrow of the present is already forgotten in the joy of anticipation. Something of the same kind happened during King's speech, as his hearers were caught up into the exhilaration of the freedom he glimpsed: 'At that moment it seemed as if the Kingdom of God appeared. But it only lasted a moment' (Coretta King).[25]

Both dreams were wrung from and given in the pain of the present. The German theologian Jürgen Moltmann, whose book *Theology of Hope* did so much to restore the dimension of hope to theology in general and to Christian political involvement in particular, traces his theology back to the root experience of God he had in prisoner of war camps in 1945—8, when the psalms helped him perceive the presence of God with him in the darkness:

> This experience of not sinking into the abyss but of being held up from afar was the beginning of a clear hope, without which it is impossible to live at all. At the same time, even this hope cut two ways; on the one hand it provided the strength to get up again after every inward or outward defeat; on the other hand it made the soul rub itself raw on the barbed wire, making it impossible to settle down in captivity or come to terms with it.[26]

So for oppressed people hopeful dreams of the future are freedom's protest against the pain of the present. Discovery of God in the darkness—the experience of the psalmists—must at the same time be the gift of hope. As God's light breaks into the darkness, the darkness can be seen to be a tunnel, the light at the end already visible.

In the psalm the moment of visionary exhilaration passes but remains the inspiration of prayer: 'Restore our fortunes, O LORD' (v. 4a). From the God who creates light in the darkness can be expected an event as miraculous and as natural as the seasonal flooding of the dry wadi beds in the southern desert (v. 4b). For ancient people, such annual events, like the cycle of sowing and harvesting (vv. 5—6), were God's annual gift of life to dead nature. Sowing seed was a kind of burial (cf. John 12.24), prior to rebirth or resurrection, and so traditionally associated with weeping,[27] just as harvest is naturally accompanied by joy (vv. 5—6). Thus the metaphor of sowing and reaping *both* gives meaning to present, sorrowful experience *and* anticipates the future as deliverance by God. The human activity of sowing is, after all, necessary, if there is to be a harvest, but it is God who gives the harvest (1 Cor. 3.6—7) and its accompanying joy.

Thus, when the psalm returns from the joy of the dream to the pain of the present, it is with a new perspective on the pain. The desolate present itself offers no hope. But in the light of the hope given by God, it can be seen as the time of sowing which must precede the time of reaping. 'It is faith in the miraculous life-giving power of God which transfigures the sufferings of the present time . . . To that faith is revealed a hidden divine law: sowing in tears and reaping in joy are inseparable.'[28] That law, of course, was enacted in the passion and resurrection of Jesus (cf. John 16.20−2).

Martin Luther King again, in the same speech:

> I am not unmindful that some of you have come here out of excessive trials and tribulation. Some of you have come fresh from narrow jail cells. Some of you have come from areas where your quest for freedom left you battered by the storms of persecution and staggered by the winds of police brutality. You have been the veterans of creative suffering. Continue to work with the faith that unearned suffering is redemptive.
>
> Go back to Mississippi; go back to Alabama; go back to South Carolina; go back to Georgia; go back to Louisiana; go back to the slums and ghettos of the northern cities, knowing that somehow this situation can, and will, be changed.[29]

The Namibian Version

Zephania Kameeta, whose original psalm of complaint we have already quoted, also writes versions of the biblical psalms—very free versions in which he gives new, contextual expression to the fundamental meaning of the psalms. His version of Psalm 126 follows the usual interpretation of verse 1b (rather than the understanding of 'dream' as 'prophetic vision', suggested above) but catches the prophetic sense of verses 1−4, as well as the way in which anticipated joy invades present suffering:

When the day comes on which our victory
   will shine like a torch in the night,
   it will be like a dream.
We will laugh and sing for joy.
Then the other nations will say about us,
   'The Lord did great things for them.'
Indeed, he is doing great things for us;
that is why we are happy in our suffering.

Lord, break the chains of humiliation and death,
   just as on that glorious morning
   when you were raised.

71

Let those who weep as they sow the seeds of justice and freedom,
gather the harvest of peace and reconciliation.

Those who weep as they go out as instruments of your love
   will come back singing with joy,
   as they will witness the disappearance of hate
and the manifestation of your love in your world.[30]

5: Taxing Questions

Jesus on Taxation

Jesus' answer to the question about the tribute money (Mark 12.13—17) has frequently been treated as the *locus classicus* for Jesus' view of politics, and far-reaching conclusions (about, for example, Church—state relations) have been drawn from it. This is not entirely unjustified. It *is* one—though only one—of Jesus' most explicit comments on political matters, and it is a comment on that aspect of politics—taxation—through which the political sphere impinged most noticeably on Jesus' contemporaries. Unfortunately, however, the passage has too often been interpreted outside its contexts in the political situation of Jesus' time and in the teaching of Jesus as a whole. Moreover, the other occasion on which Jesus talked about taxation (Matt. 17.24—7) has been widely neglected and rarely related to his comment on paying tribute to Caesar.[1]

In this chapter we shall study these two passages and examine their teaching in relation to each other and in relation to Jesus' teaching as a whole. In particular, we shall see how an understanding of their context in the political situation of the time is essential to their accurate exegesis.

The Temple Tax

Matthew 17.24—7[2]

24 When [Jesus and his disciples] arrived in Capernaum, the
   collectors of the half-shekel tax went up to Peter and said,
25 'Does not your teacher pay the half-shekel tax?' He said, 'Yes.'
   And when he entered the house, Jesus was the first to speak.
   'What do you think, Simon?,' he asked. 'From whom do the
   kings of the earth take toll or tribute? From their sons or from
26 the others?' And when he said, 'From the others,' Jesus said to
27 him, 'Then the sons are exempt. But so that we may not offend
   them [the tax-collectors], go to the lake and cast a line. Take

the first fish that comes up, open its mouth, and you will find a shekel. Take it and give it to them for me and for yourself.'

The tax in question here was the temple tax, a half-shekel payable annually by every adult male Jew. It was levied by the temple authorities themselves to finance the public sacrificial worship in the temple in Jerusalem. The tax was probably of fairly recent origin, but the Pharisees and the Sadducean priestly aristocracy who ran the temple regarded it as a tax instituted by Moses, on the basis of Exodus 30.11−16 (cf. Exod. 38.25−6). However, this interpretation of Exodus 30.11−16 was denied by some Jews at the time of Jesus, who denied the obligation to pay an annual half-shekel to the temple. The fact that the legitimacy of the tax was debated may explain the tax-collectors' question to Peter (v. 24): they are checking that Jesus admits liability to the tax. It is important to notice that the temple tax was regarded as a tax, not a voluntary contribution, and was legally required at the same rate from all adult males, with no allowance for poverty. Furthermore, it was conceived very directly as a tax levied by and paid to *God*. It was part and parcel of the concept of Israel as a theocracy governed in God's name by the temple authorities. It would be a mistake to regard this tax as, in modern terms, an ecclesiastical *rather than* political matter, for Israel was a religio-political entity in which such distinctions were only relative. The chief priests and the Sanhedrin were the Jewish government, ruling in God's name and, as it happened, also in collaboration with the Roman overlords.

Precisely what Jesus meant by his question to Peter in verse 25 is debated. Some think the point is that kings do not tax their own nation ('their sons') but foreign subject peoples. The reference would then be to an imperialist policy of exploiting an empire for the benefit of the ruling nation. But in that case, we should have to suppose that Jesus is exaggerating in order to make his point, for it was not generally true in the ancient world that kings exempted their own nation from taxation. In the case of the Roman Empire, for example, although much the largest part of the burden of taxation fell on the subject nations, such as the Jews, Roman citizens did pay taxes. In terms of the two types of taxation Jesus mentions, they paid indirect taxes ('toll') but not direct taxes ('tribute'). It has also been suggested that by the king's 'sons' Jesus refers to the king's household (his employees and top administrators), who did not pay taxes because they were maintained at the king's expense. However, this is not the natural sense of his words, and it seems best to take 'sons' quite literally: kings do not tax their own children, but only the rest of their subjects.

Jesus is here using the analogy between God's rule and the rule of earthly kings in a way which is entirely characteristic of his teaching. His argument is that, if we are going to compare the way God, the heavenly king, rules his people with the way earthly kings rule their peoples, the proper analogy is not with the way earthly kings treat their *subjects* but with the way they treat their own *children*. Characteristically, Jesus sees God's fatherhood as the key to the nature of his rule. God's rule over his people is not really like that of an earthly king; it is more like that of an earthly father. So just as even kings do not tax their own children, so God, who is a father to his people, does not tax them. (Jesus is not here distinguishing some of God's people, who have the special privilege of 'sons', from others, whom he does tax. The 'sons' are all of God's people. Jesus' teaching assumes that sonship is the *status* of Israel as a nation (Mark 7.27; Matt. 8.12; 15.26), while Jesus' mission was to call Israel to *fulfil* that status in a renewed Israel of which his disciples were the nucleus.)

Thus Jesus' objection is to *theocratic* taxation, taxing God's people in God's name, because it is inconsistent with the way Jesus understands the rule of God. (The early Church seems to have taken the point. Notice how carefully, in 2 Cor. 8–9, Paul avoids any suggestion that Christian giving is anything like taxation.) Jesus in fact pays the temple tax in order 'not to give offence' to the tax-collectors. These would have been local people who undertook the task as an act of piety, and they could easily have taken Jesus' refusal to pay as a criticism of the sacrificial worship in the temple which the tax supported. But Jesus' method of payment, embarrassing as most modern commentators find it, is designed to reinforce his point. The miracle shows that God is not like a king who exacts money from his subjects, but, quite the contrary, like a father who provides for his children's needs. Instead of demanding a temple shekel from Peter, God actually provides him with one.

The Realities of Taxation

Jesus' attitude to taxation in this passage is strikingly negative. If

75

God does not tax his people, the implication is that taxation is, to say the least, a less than ideal instrument of government. Jesus does not deny the right of earthly kings to tax their subjects, but he does suggest that in this respect their rule is not at all like God's.

This negative attitude to taxation is not surprising. The burden of taxation was the principal reason why ordinary people in Jesus' time felt their government to be oppressive. Jews felt this as much about Herodian rule as about direct Roman rule, and in fact Herod Antipas's taxes in Galilee may have been a greater burden than the Roman taxes in Judaea. Taxation was especially burdensome for Jews, because in addition to these civil taxes they were also liable to the theocratic taxes imposed by the Jewish religious authorities: the annual tithe and other forms of priestly dues, for the support of the priests and Levites, the 'second tithe' payable every third year, for the support of the poor, and the annual half-shekel temple tax. Moreover, since the temple tax was intended to finance the daily sacrificial worship in the temple, the various forms of obligatory sacrificial offerings cannot be in principle distinguished from taxation. To the ordinary person struggling to meet these demands, the temple theocracy could easily seem just another level of oppressive government, and to a large extent, in the hands of the priestly aristocracy who ran the temple, it was. The conspicuous wealth of the high priestly families was widely resented and connected with their control of the temple finances, of which the temple tax was the most important source. In other words, the taxes levied in God's name, for his worship, benefited the theocratic ruling class, the Sadducean aristocracy, at the expense of the people. In this respect they were no different from the taxes of 'the kings of the earth'.

It is important to remember that taxation in the ancient world could not normally be perceived by the ordinary people who bore the main burden of it as having anything to do with their benefit. Taxation benefited the rulers, not the ruled. High-minded Roman governors, in the best tradition of the Roman civil service, might genuinely see the *Pax Romana* as Rome's gift to the world, much as the Victorians viewed the British Empire. In the Roman civil-service view, the taxation the Romans levied was required for the maintenance of the Empire's military power and bureaucratic structure, in other words for the peace and security with which the subjects of the Empire were blessed by Roman rule. This view was easily shared by the local ruling classes, such as the priestly aristocracy in Jerusalem, who collaborated with the Roman authorities and benefited from Roman rule. But it was, of course, a view which served to cover a good deal of exploitation and was not likely to convince the exploited.[3] For many of the subject peoples of the Empire, taxation was both an economic burden and a sign of their subjection. The Jews, with the cynicism characteristic of alienated subjects, said that the Romans built fine bridges simply in order to be able to collect tolls for the use of them![4] Authoritarian rule, in the style of the master—slave relationship, is usually perceived by its subjects as exploitative (cf. 1 Sam. 8.10—18), and they are very often right. Under the governments of Jesus' time, being liable to taxation meant being subject to exploitation by others.

In this respect, Jesus' negative attitude to taxation coheres with his view of contemporary government in other sayings. He took it for granted, as a view which the ordinary people of his time shared, that government was oppressive: 'You know that those who are supposed to rule over the Gentiles lord it over them, and their great men exercise authority over them. But it shall not be so among you . . .' (Mark 10.42—3; cf. Luke 22.25—6). Jesus here contrasts the authoritarian political rule of his day with how things are done under God's rule. In Matthew 17.25—6, Jesus has the same concern. The temple tax, which as a poll-tax weighed heavily on the poor, was levied by God, and therefore represented God as an oppressive despot, exploiting his people. But God's rule is not like that!

Jesus' Demonstration in the Temple

Our investigation of Jesus' attitude to the temple tax in Matthew 17.24—7 can also help us to understand that incident in his career which is commonly known as the cleansing of the temple, but might be better called Jesus' demonstration in the temple, since it was a kind of prophetic act of protest against what was going on in the temple court (Mark 11.15—17).[5] One element in this protest was Jesus' act of overturning the tables of the money-changers.

The money-changers were present in the temple court at that time, just before Passover, because this was the period in which the temple tax had to be paid and money-changers were needed to change money into the correct currency (the so-called 'temple shekels') for paying the tax. The money-changing was not a piece of private enterprise going on in the temple precincts, but a facility organized by the temple treasury and no doubt operated by members of the temple staff. Jesus attacked the tables of the money-changers because they were the most visible manifestation of the temple's tax-collecting operation. He was not implying, as has sometimes been suggested, that the money-changing should not be allowed within the sacred precincts but might properly go on elsewhere. Nor was he suggesting, as is frequently supposed, that the money-changers were swindling their customers and making a dishonest profit. His objection was to the tax itself, which the money-changing facilitated, and to those who ran the temple's tax-collecting operation in God's name.

The overturning of the tables of the money-changers was one of several acts of protest which Jesus made against the financial business of the temple (Mark 11.15—16; cf. also John 2.14—16). This helps us to see his objection to the temple tax as part of a larger protest against the way the priestly aristocracy were running the finances of the temple as a profit-making business, so that, instead of facilitating worship, they were laying oppressive economic burdens on the people—and all in the name of *God's* rule over his people. It is significant that among the commercial operations which Jesus temporarily disrupted, special mention is made of the sale of doves as sacrificial offerings (Mark 11.15; Matt. 21.12). Doves were the sacrifices of the poor. In a few cases doves were the type of offering required of everyone (Lev. 15.14, 29; Num. 6.10), but in most cases they were an alternative form of offering for those who could not afford the more expensive sacrificial animals. This was true not only of voluntary offerings (Lev. 1.14), but also of certain types of obligatory offerings (Lev. 5.7; 12.6—8; 14.22), and therefore dove offerings could approximate, for the poor, to another kind of theocratic tax. A poor person would probably only rarely sacrifice an animal other than a dove, but would quite frequently sacrifice doves. What drew Jesus' criticism, however, was not the sacrificial system itself, but the fact that the temple operated a monopoly in the sale of doves certified fit for sacrifice, and was therefore able to keep the price high, for the benefit of the temple treasury. In other words, the laws which were specifically designed to make worship possible for the poor, by prescribing a cheaper form of offering, were being so applied as to make them a financial burden on the poor.

Jesus' comment on the situation (Mark 11.17) aptly contrasts God's intention for the temple, declared in Scripture, with what the temple authorities had made it. The temple was meant to be 'a house of prayer' (Isa. 56.7): the place of God's gracious accessibility to all his people, whose sacrificial worship was to be a vehicle of their prayer. But the priestly aristocracy had made it 'a cave of brigands' (Jer. 7.11): so to speak, the base from which they plundered the people. They were frustrating the real purpose of the sacrificial cult and turning it instead into a means of financial exaction. As a result God's rule was being represented as only too similar to the kingdoms of the Gentiles. Instead of the fatherly God who provides for his people, the God whom the poor found represented by the temple authorities was a sanction for economic oppression.

Tribute to Caesar

Mark 12.13–17 (RSV)

13 And they sent to him some of the Pharisees and some of the
14 Herodians, to entrap him in his talk. And they came and said to him, 'Teacher, we know that you are true, and care for no man; for you do not regard the position of men, but truly teach the way of God. Is it lawful to pay taxes to Caesar, or not?
15 Should we pay them, or should we not?' But knowing their hypocrisy, he said to them, 'Why put me to the test? Bring me a
16 coin and let me look at it.' And they brought one. And he said to them, 'Whose likeness and inscription is this?' They said to
17 him, 'Caesar's.' Jesus said to them, 'Render to Caesar the things that are Caesar's, and to God the things that are God's.' And they were amazed at him.

Here the tax in question was the second type of tax to which Jesus referred in Matthew 17.25. It was the tribute, a form of direct taxation payable to Rome in provinces under direct Roman rule, and therefore payable at this time in Judaea, but not in Galilee. As such, it brought home to Jews, in a particularly irksome way, their subjection to pagan rule, especially as the tax had to be paid in Roman coins (denarii) which bore the idolatrous image of the pagan Emperor.[6]

At first sight it seems hard to square Jesus' attitude to this Roman tax with his attitude to the temple tax. Whereas he had rejected theocratic taxation as inappropriate to God's rule, he seems here to accept the legitimacy of Roman taxation, ignoring its oppressive character. But at this point it becomes very important to appreciate the polemical context in which the Pharisees and the Herodians asked their trick question. Since the revolt of Judas the Galilean in AD 6 (Acts 5.37), when the tribute to Caesar was first imposed on Judaea, there had been Jewish opposition to Roman taxation not only on economic, but on religio-political grounds. The Zealot[7] argument was that Israel and her land belonged to God, and God alone was the legitimate ruler of his people. Caesar had no rightful sovereignty over the people of God. Taxes paid to Caesar were an acknowledgement of his lordship, a token of submission to slavery, and should therefore be withheld. By thus combining resentment of foreign rule and objection to the burden of taxation into a form of religious nationalism, the Zealot movement made the payment of tribute to Caesar the most likely basis of popular support for revolt against Rome.[8]

Jesus' enemies clearly hoped to elicit from him an opinion sympathetic to the Zealot view, which to Roman ears would be very dangerously seditious (cf. Luke 23.2). That they hoped for this may have been due, not only to the fact that Jesus, like the Zealots, talked about the coming of God's Kingdom, but also to the fact that his occasional references to pagan government were far from favourable (Matt. 17.25; Mark 10.42).

Jesus' reply, however, is a directly anti-Zealot one: that God's claim on his people does not conflict with Caesar's right to receive taxation. He makes this point in an argument which really comprises two stages. The first is to the effect that what bears Caesar's image obviously belongs to him and should be given back to him. This is more a rhetorical than a strictly logical argument. It cannot strictly prove the point, though it has a kind of *ad hominem* value. But it is significant in view of the strict Jewish sensibility to the idolatrous nature of the image on the coin. I do not think Jesus means that a coin which thus contravenes the law of God belongs to Gentiles and should therefore be given back to them.[9] The issue of idolatry was more serious than that. For the Zealots, the idolatrous nature of the coin pointed to the more fundamental idolatry of Caesar's claim to taxation: by taxing God's people Caesar was usurping God's sovereignty. Thus to render tribute to Caesar in his idolatrous coinage was to acknowledge his blasphemous claim to a right which was really God's alone. But Jesus deliberately leaves the whole issue of idolatry out of account. For him the image on the coin has a quite different significance: it

is a mark of legitimate ownership which points to Caes
legitimate right to tax his Jewish subjects.

The second element in Jesus' argument is the distinction he
makes, in some sense, between Caesar's rights and God's rights.
This the Zealots refused to do. For them God's rights over his
people were exclusive, rendering Caesar's claims illegitimate. Jesus,
on the other hand, takes up an Old Testament distinction between
'the things of God' and 'the things of the king' (1 Chron. 26.32, cf.
26.30; 2 Chron. 19.11),[10] thereby demonstrating that Scripture
does not support the Zealot view. This Old Testament background
to Jesus' clinching epigram seems to me conclusive against those
who try to read the saying in some other way, as not endorsing
Caesar's right to taxation.[11] It should be noticed that Jesus is ready
to apply to Caesar the phrase which in the Old Testament referred
to a Jewish king. In Jesus' view a pagan Emperor had as much
right to taxation as a native Jewish ruler. If this put him out of step
with contemporary Jewish nationalism, it was not inconsistent
with the Old Testament, which never opposes the tribute imposed
on Judaea by the Babylonian and Persian Empires.[12]

Once we recognize the extent to which Jesus' pronouncement is
polemically aimed against the Zealot view, it is clear that he is
making only a limited point. He is not making an absolute
demarcation between Caesar's sphere of authority and that of
God, as though political affairs were not subject to God. This
possibility is unlikely to have occurred to Jesus or his Jewish
hearers, who would have taken it for granted that God's law
applies to the whole of life. The two Old Testament phrases Jesus
uses make a pragmatic, not a general theological, distinction
between 'the things of God' and 'the things of the king'. Jesus'
point is not that God has no rights over Caesar, but that God's
rights do not *exclude* Caesar's. Of course, Caesar's exercise of his
right to taxation might on occasions conflict with God's law—he
might exceed his right—but the right itself was allowed by God's
law. This is the only point Jesus intends to make.

Thus Jesus' assertion has little in common with modern claims
that the Church should not meddle in politics. But it does reject a
kind of theocratic politics which was popular among some Jews in
Jesus' day. Discussions of Jesus and the Zealots frequently give
the impression that political violence was the main point of
difference between them. But our passage may help us to see that
the difference was in fact a broader one.

81

Jesus and Jewish Politics

From a comparison of Jesus' teaching in the two cases we have studied—the temple tax and the tribute to Caesar—some interesting results emerge. Jesus' primary objection is to theocratic politics, whether this takes the form of taxation by the temple authorities in the name of God's sovereignty over his people, or whether it takes the form of Zealot opposition to Roman taxes in the name of God's sovereignty over his people. Jesus' teaching in the case of the temple tax can give us a clue to his opposition to the Zealots in the case of tribute to Caesar. According to Jesus, God does not rule his people in the way that earthly kings rule. He does not, for example, treat them as subjects who owe him taxes. But this kind of distinction was not really the concern of the Zealots, who were simply trying to transfer sovereignty, including the right to taxation, from Caesar to God. Presumably a Zealot government would not be so very different from Caesar's government *except* that it would be a Jewish government ruling in the name of Israel's God. Thus theocratic policies, as advocated by Jesus' Jewish contemporaries, do not implement the rule of God as Jesus understood it. They are more a way of using 'God' as an ideological justification for ordinary political ends, in the case of the Zealots for national sovereignty. In the end this is not so different from Caesar's own claim to divinity.

Jesus certainly saw Roman rule as oppressive—his critical remarks about the kings of the Gentiles leave no doubt of that—and no one who cared about the ordinary people of first-century Palestine as Jesus did could have failed to do so. But for Jesus the issue was not whether Jews or Gentiles ruled. The real issue was the nature of God's rule over his people, and therefore the target of his attack when he reached Jerusalem had to be, not Pilate, but the temple authorities, the official heads of the Jewish theocracy, who misrepresented God's rule as oppressive and used God's rule as a sanction for their own oppressive power.

Of course, Gentile rule was oppressive: Jesus hardly needed to make the point. The point he felt the need to make, however, was that God's people, under God's rule, should be *different* from the Gentiles. If Jews love only their fellow Jews and hate their national enemies, they are no different from Gentiles (Matt. 5.43—7). If God's people are primarily concerned with material security and prosperity, they are no different from the Gentiles (Matt. 6.32). If the potential leaders of God's people vie for power and prestige, they are no better than the kings of the Gentiles (Mark 10.42—4). God's rule is radically different from that of the kings of the earth, and therefore life in accordance with God's rule will be different from the general run of human affairs. It will reflect God's fatherly care for his people and his non-discriminating concern for all people (Matt. 5.45). It will be characterized by radical trust in God's provision (Matt. 6.25—33), sacrificial service for others (Mark 10.43—5) and love for enemies (Matt. 5.38—47).

The various Jewish political options of Jesus' day were no more concerned with these values than was the Roman government. A change of government would have done little to further God's rule as Jesus understood it. A radical change of heart, renewing the fundamental relationship of God's people to their God, was Jesus' priority. But it does not follow that such a change of heart would be irrelevant to politics.

No Taxation without . . .
Clearly Jesus was far from giving wholehearted approval to the Roman Empire's system of taxation. The imposition of taxes on subject nations is quite unlike the rule of God. It could be no part of that imitation of God's ways which Jesus enjoins on his followers (Matt. 5.45, 48). But on the other hand, Jesus did not deny Caesar's right to levy taxes. God's law permits it because human government without taxation would be impossible.

This double attitude of Jesus to taxation—rejecting the notion that God taxes his people, while accepting the legitimacy of civil taxation—recurs in Paul, who accepted the right of the Roman government to tax its subjects, including Christians (Rom. 13.6—7), while taking great care to describe his collection for the Christian poor of Jerusalem in terms which distinguished it from a tax. The collection's value, he insists, depends on its voluntary character; it is a matter not of constraint but of love; each individual must decide for himself the amount of his gift (Rom. 15.26—7; 2 Cor. 8.3—5, 8; 9.5, 7). We may also note that the purpose of the collection—redistribution of wealth for the sake of the poor (2 Cor. 8.14)—also reflects the nature of God's rule better than most forms of contemporary taxation, which tended to benefit the ruling classes at the expense of the poor. Paul's collection illustrates rather well what might take the place of taxation in Jesus' understanding of the Kingdom of God.

In Jesus' time and Paul's the ideal of life under God's rule and the approximation to it in the life of Jesus' disciples could only be set critically against the political systems of the day. But is there therefore an *inevitable* gulf between human government and the rule of God? Or is it possible for human government to reflect the principles of God's rule to some degree?

Human governments cannot *be* the rule of God. Theocratic politics, in that sense, are a dangerous illusion. A government which presumes to be the rule of God is almost bound to absolutize itself, to deny the moral ambiguities of its policies and practice, to reject criticism and to suppress dissent, and to lose its ideals in self-justifying oppression. Good government requires the recognition of fallible human limits. It requires humble remembrance of the gap between itself and the Kingdom of God. So claims to theocracy always need to be countered by stressing, as Jesus did, the contrasts between the ways of God and the empirical facts of actual human governments.

But while resisting the temptation to theocracy, human governments, or Christians involved in human government, can try to imitate the principles of God's rule so far as circumstances and the hardness of human hearts allow. They cannot abolish taxation and rely on voluntary gifts, as God does. But they can get much closer than Caesar's government did to an ideal situation in which those who pay taxes do so willingly, as a fair contribution to the common good. While human hearts are sinful, those unwilling to contribute to the common good will always experience taxation as a constraint. But where taxation is seen to benefit not the ruling classes but all, and especially those in need, where it is assessed in a recognizably equitable way,[13] and where, in a democratic system, its administration is responsible to the people, then it need not be a form of social exploitation but can approximate to a form of social love.

6: The Fallen City

Revelation 18

Attitudes to the Roman Empire in the New Testament writings vary according to the circumstances of the Church at the time and place of writing. But from a fairly early stage of Christian history there was sporadic conflict provoked by the Roman state's demand for absolute political loyalty expressed in religious form as worship of the Roman Emperor and the traditional gods of Rome. This demand met the Christian refusal to acknowledge any absolute lordship other than Christ's. The inevitability of this conflict with the state is seen most clearly in the book of Revelation, which uses the literary form of the apocalypse to uncover the deep religious truth of the political situation in the late first century. A remarkable feature of the book is that it is far from confining its criticism of Rome to the issue of Rome's persecution of Christians, but sees this issue as bringing to the surface evils which were deeply rooted in the whole system of Roman imperial power. This feature makes Revelation one of the fiercest attacks on Rome and one of the most effective pieces of political resistance literature from the period of the early Roman empire. We shall take chapter 18 as a sample of Revelation's critique of Rome.

Revelation 18 (RSV)

1   After this I saw another angel coming down from heaven,
     having great authority; and the earth was made bright with
2   his splendour. And he called out with a mighty voice,
       'Fallen, fallen is Babylon the great!
       It has become a dwelling place of demons,
       a haunt of every foul spirit,
       a haunt of every foul and hateful bird;
3   for all nations have drunk the wine of her impure passion,
       and the kings of the earth have committed fornication
          with her,
       and the merchants of the earth have grown rich with the
          wealth of her wantonness.'

4 Then I heard another voice from heaven saying,
  'Come out of her, my people,
  lest you take part in her sins,
  lest you share in her plagues;
5 for her sins are heaped high as heaven,
  and God has remembered her iniquities.
6 Render to her as she herself has rendered,
  and repay her double for her deeds;
  mix a double draught for her in the cup she mixed.
7 As she glorified herself and played the wanton,
  so give her a like measure of torment and mourning.
  Since in her heart she says, "A queen I sit,
  I am no widow, mourning I shall never see,"
8 so shall her plagues come in a single day,
  pestilence and mourning and famine,
  and she shall be burned with fire;
  for mighty is the Lord God who judges her.'
9 And the kings of the earth, who committed fornication and
  were wanton with her, will weep and wail over her when they
10 see the smoke of her burning; they will stand far off, in fear of
  her torment, and say,
  'Alas! alas! thou great city,
  thou mighty city, Babylon!
  In one hour has thy judgment come.'
11 And the merchants of the earth weep and mourn for her, since
12 no one buys their cargo any more, cargo of gold, silver, jewels
  and pearls, fine linen, purple, silk and scarlet, all kinds of
  scented wood, all articles of ivory, all articles of costly wood,
13 bronze, iron and marble, cinnamon, spice, incense, myrrh,
  frankincense, wine, oil, fine flour and wheat, cattle and sheep,
  horses and chariots, and slaves, that is, human souls.
14 'The fruit for which thy soul longed has gone from thee,
  and all thy dainties and thy splendour are lost to thee, never
  to be found again!'
15 The merchants of these wares, who gained wealth from her,
  will stand far off, in fear of her torment, weeping and mourning aloud,
16 'Alas, alas, for the great city
  that was clothed in fine linen, in purple and scarlet,
  bedecked with gold, with jewels, and with pearls!

17 In one hour all this wealth has been laid waste.'
And all shipmasters and seafaring men, sailors and all whose
18 trade is on the sea, stood far off and cried out as they saw the
smoke of her burning,
'What city was like the great city?'
19 And they threw dust on their heads, as they wept and
mourned, crying out,
'Alas, alas, for the great city
where all who had ships at sea grew rich by her wealth!
In one hour she has been laid waste.'
20 'Rejoice over her, O heaven,
O saints and apostles and prophets,
for God has given judgment for you against her!'
21 Then a mighty angel took up a stone like a great millstone and
threw it into the sea, saying,
'So shall Babylon the great city be thrown down with
violence,
and shall be found no more;
22 and the sound of harpers and minstrels, of flute players and
trumpeters,
shall be heard in thee no more;
and a craftsman of any craft
shall be found in thee no more;
and the sound of the millstone
shall be heard in thee no more;
23 and the light of a lamp
shall shine in thee no more;
and the voice of bridegroom and bride
shall be heard in thee no more;
for thy merchants were the great men of the earth,
and all nations were deceived by thy sorcery.'
24 And in her was found the blood of prophets and of saints and
of all who have been slain on earth.

Rome as Beast and Harlot
The book of Revelation uses two major, complementary images of
the evil power of Rome. One is the sea-monster ('the beast'),
introduced in chapter 13. It represents the imperial power, the
Roman Emperors as a political institution, and in particular their
military might, on which the Roman Empire was founded. The

other image is of the great city Babylon, first named in 14.8, and then portrayed as a woman, 'the great harlot', in chapter 17. Babylon is the city of Rome (built on seven hills: 17.9), and in particular the city of Rome as a *corrupting influence* on the peoples of the Empire. Chapter 17 brings the two images together: the harlot is enthroned on the seven heads of the beast (17.3, 9–10). In other words, Roman civilization, as a corrupting influence, rides on the back of Roman military power. The city of Rome grew great through military conquest, which brought wealth and power to the city, and its economic and cultural influence spread through the world in the wake of the imperial armies.

John never forgets that Rome's power is founded on war and conquest, but he also recognizes that it cannot be reduced to this. As well as the irresistible military might of the beast, there are the deceptive wiles of the great harlot. It is on the latter that we shall focus in this chapter.

The satanic, antichristian nature of Roman power, as exercised in John's time, was demonstrated most obviously by the Roman state religion, in which the power of the state was deified and its worship required of all subjects. It may be that John's use of the two distinct images of Roman power—the beast and the harlot city—was assisted by a feature of this state religion. It included not only the worship of the divinized Emperors but also the worship of the goddess Roma, who was a kind of personification of the city of Rome. It may be that in the woman of Revelation 17 John's readers would have recognized the goddess Roma,[1] revealed by the vision in her true character: a Roman prostitute, wearing her name on a headband on her forehead (17.5) as prostitutes did in the streets of Rome.[2]

John describes the impulse to the imperial cult in 13.4: people 'worshipped the beast saying, "Who is like the beast, and who can fight against it?"' The irresistible military might of Rome seems divine and attracts worship. The verse has a kind of parallel in 18.18, with reference to Babylon. Those who there lament her downfall cry, 'What city was like the great city?' Here the wealth and splendour of the city of Rome evoke admiration, just as her military might evoked spontaneous, if somewhat craven, worship. The point should not be pressed too far. If the picture of the great harlot owes something to the goddess Roma, John does not actually portray her as an object of worship, as he does the beast. His point is more that, through her corrupting influence, she promotes the

88

idolatrous religion of Rome. But Babylon comes close to self-deification in her proud boast, 'A queen I sit, I am no widow, mourning I shall never see' (18.7), which echoes not only ancient Babylon's boast (Isaiah 47.7−8) but also contemporary Rome's self-promoted reputation as the eternal city.[3] It was the city which believed, as an article of faith, that she could never fall, whose fall is announced in Revelation 18.

The Delusion of the Pax Romana

John recognizes that many of Rome's subjects welcomed and appreciated her rule. The supposed benefits of Rome's rule were promoted through the imperial propaganda by means of the famous phrase *Pax Romana*—the Roman peace. Rome was supposed to have given to the Mediterranean world unity, stability, security, the conditions of prosperity. As a grateful inscription at Halicarnassus, which celebrates the Emperor Augustus as 'saviour of the whole human race', put it:

> Land and sea have peace, the cities flourish under a good legal system, in harmony and with an abundance of food, there is an abundance of all good things, people are filled with happy hopes for the future and with delight at the present.[4]

From John's prophetic perspective, however, these apparent benefits are not what they seem: they are the favours of a prostitute, bought at a high price.

The image of the harlot is fundamental to John's understanding of Rome. Even when he is speaking primarily of the city, as in chapter 18, he does not forget that the city is a harlot. Hence the terms of the description in 17.1−6 are echoed in 18.3 (cf. 17.2) and 18.16 (cf. 18.4). The basic notion, of course, is that those who associate with a harlot pay her for the privilege. And Rome is no ordinary harlot: she is a rich courtesan, whose expensive clothes and jewellery (17.4) indicate the luxurious lifestyle she maintains at her lovers' expense. The meaning of the picture is unpacked for us when the harlot's clothing and jewels are described again, in the same terms, in 18.16. Here they are plainly a metaphor for the wealth of the city of Rome, for all the luxury goods listed in 18.12−13, brought to Rome by the great network of trade throughout her empire. In other words, Rome is a harlot because her associations with the peoples of her empire are for her own economic benefit. The *Pax Romana* is really a system of economic exploitation of the empire. For the favours of Rome—the security and prosperity of the *Pax Romana*—her lovers pay a high price. Her subjects give far more to her than she gives to them.

There are, of course, those who have a vested interest in the power and the economic dominance of Rome: the kings, the merchants and the mariners (18.9—19). To these people, who share in Rome's profit, we shall return later. But many of Rome's subjects are in fact exploited by her, yet fail to see it. They are taken in by Roman propaganda. They are dazzled by Rome's glory and seduced by the promised benefits of the *Pax Romana*. This delusion John portrays by means of two additional metaphors, which extend the harlot image. When he refers to the harlot's influence, not on the ruling classes of the empire, but over the peoples of the empire, he says that she intoxicates them with the wine of her fornication (14.8; 17.2; 18.3) or that she deceives them with her sorceries (18.23). The latter probably refers to the magic arts used by a prostitute to entice her clients (as in Nahum 3.4), or may simply portray Rome in another guise: as a witch (cf. Isaiah 47.12). In any case, it is clear what John means. When Rome's subjects, the ordinary people of the empire, welcome her rule, it is because she has enticed and seduced them. They are taken in by the prostitute's wiles and the tricks of her trade.

We have seen, then, that the primary meaning of the harlot image in Revelation 17—18 is economic. This is in line with one Old Testament source of the image: Isaiah 23.15—18, where Tyre is called a harlot. The reference there is obviously to the vast trading activity through which the city of Tyre had grown rich. Tyre's commercial enterprise is compared with prostitution because it is association with other nations for the sake of profit. Very likely John had this passage in mind, since, as we shall see, his prophecy of the fall of Babylon draws not only on Old Testament oracles against Babylon but also on Old Testament oracles against Tyre. But he must also have been aware of a much more common Old Testament use of harlotry as a metaphor.[5] In this usage, idolatrous religion is described as harlotry, because the people of God, when they adopted pagan religious practices, were being unfaithful to their husband, God, and 'played the harlot' with other gods (e.g. Jeremiah 3). This Old Testament sense of harlotry could strictly be applied only to the people of God, but it is very likely that John takes advantage of the traditional association of harlotry with idolatrous religion, when he refers to the *corrupting* influence of the harlot city (19.2). When the intoxicating draught from her golden cup is otherwise described as 'abominations and the impurities of her fornication' (17.4), and when she is described as 'the mother [i.e. the mother-city, the metropolis] of harlots and of the abominations of the earth' (17.5), the reference, following a familiar Old Testament use of the term 'abominations', is to idolatrous religion. Of course, Rome could not be held responsible for all the idolatrous religion of her empire, most of which pre-existed her conquests. But pagan religion was inseparable from all aspects of society in the Roman Empire; it was closely bound up with the economic life of the Empire; and, in particular, the extension of Roman rule, with its supposed benefits, involved the imperial cult. Part of the delusion of the *Pax Romana*—the intoxicating wine from the harlot's cup—was the people's sense of gratitude to the Emperor, who was worshipped as a divine saviour for the blessings he had brought to his subjects. The political religion of Rome was the worst kind of false religion, since it absolutized Rome's claim on her subjects and cloaked her exploitation of them in the garb of religious loyalty. Thus, for John, Rome's economic exploitation and the corrupting influence of her state religion go hand in hand.

Rome as the Heir of Babylon and Tyre

Like the whole book of Revelation, chapter 18 is full of allusions to the Old Testament: there is scarcely a verse of the chapter in which at least one Old Testament passage is not echoed.[6] John is very conscious of writing in a long tradition of prophetic oracles, and so is constantly echoing and reapplying the oracles of his predecessors. In this chapter he creates a poetic oracle on the doom of Rome which employs the same literary forms as the Old Testament oracles from which many of its phrases and ideas come. But for John these oracles are more than a literary source. They are oracles which, because they applied to Rome's predecessors in evil, apply also to Rome.

Revelation 18 has two major Old Testament sources: Jeremiah's great oracle against Babylon (Jer. 50—1) and Ezekiel's great oracle against Tyre (Ezek. 26—8). But allusion is also made to all four of the shorter oracles against Babylon to be found in the Old Testament prophets (Isa. 13.1—14, 23; 21.1—10; 47; Jer. 25.12—38). Of course, the relevance of these Babylon oracles to Rome is already implied in John's use of the term Babylon as his cipher for Rome. No Old Testament city could more truly be called, like Rome, 'the great city which has dominion over the kings of the earth' (Rev. 17.18). Rome resembled Old Testament Babylon in being a proud, idolatrous, oppressive Empire, and especially in being the power which conquered and oppressed the people of God. Rome declared itself the heir of Babylon by setting itself against God in its political and religious policies. But it is important to notice that Ezekiel's oracle against Tyre contributes as much to Revelation 18 as Jeremiah's and Isaiah's oracles against Babylon do. The central section of the chapter, which views the fall of Babylon through the dirges sung by the kings, the merchants and the mariners (vv. 9–19), is inspired by Ezekiel's very similar picture of the fall of Tyre (Ezek. 26.15–27; 36). If Rome was the heir of Babylon in political and religious activity, she was also the heir of Tyre in economic activity. For Tyre was the greatest trading centre of the Old Testament period, who grew rich and arrogant through her commercial dealings with every part of the ancient world. Unlike Babylon, Tyre was notable, not for her political empire, but for her economic empire. So it is to focus his indictment of Rome for her *economic* exploitation and his pronouncement of judgement on Rome for *this* aspect of her evil, that John reapplies to Rome Ezekiel's oracle against Tyre. The Old Testament background therefore helps us to see how central the economic theme is to the condemnation of Rome in Revelation 18.

Recognizing the Old Testament background to the chapter can also help us in other ways to see the significance and relevance of the passage. It shows us how prophecy, whether in the Old or the New Testament, can be both very specific in its condemnation of societies contemporary with the prophet, but also paradigmatic and so available for reapplication to later societies guilty of similar evils. As we shall see, John's condemnation of Rome's commercial activity is remarkably concrete and specific, in spite of its use of Old Testament language. John perceives Rome not just as a second Tyre, but in its own precise contemporary reality. Had he not done so, his prophetic attack could not have hit its mark.

Yet at the same time he can redirect Old Testament prophecies, which found their own specific targets in Old Testament history, to a new target in contemporary Rome. The meaning of Jeremiah's oracle against Babylon was not, so to speak, exhausted when ancient Babylon fell to the armies of Cyrus of Persia. With suitable adaptation, its essential thrust found a fresh and quite appropriate object in the new Babylon of John's time. In the same way, John's own oracles transcend their application to ancient Rome. This is in fact particularly the case because John sees Rome as the culmination of all the evil empires of history. Just as the beast of Revelation 13.1–2 combines in itself the features of all four beasts of Daniel's vision (Dan. 7.3–8), so the Babylon of Revelation 18 combines in itself the evils of the two great evil cities of the prophetic oracles: Babylon and Tyre.[7] Indeed, John's Babylon is the final climax of the enterprise begun at Babel (= Babylon) in Genesis 11: the agelong human enterprise of organizing human society in opposition to God. The tower of Babel was 'only the beginning of what they will do' (Gen. 11.6); Babylon the great is the end-result. And because, in this sense, John's Babylon is inclusive of all Rome's predecessors, she is held guilty, not only of the murder of the recent victims of Roman imperialism, but of 'the blood . . . of all who have been slain on earth' (Rev. 18.24).

Thus the Babylon of Revelation is not only a specific visionary image of contemporary Rome, but also an eschatological image. In other words, it transcends its original reference and becomes a symbol of the whole history of organized human evil whose fall will be the end of history. In Revelation Babylon falls (Rev. 18) so that the new Jerusalem may descend from heaven as the capital of the eternal Kingdom of God in the new world of resurrection (Rev. 21). (The connection is clear from Rev. 19.1–8.) So just as Babylon the great includes all Rome's predecessors, so, for us, she must include all Rome's successors in the history of the world's evil empires, political, religious and economic. John's oracle against her is a cap which anyone it fits must wear.

It is therefore important to keep in view both the specific and the paradigmatic, inclusive qualities of John's prophecy. Its genius is such that it both reaches very accurately its contemporary target in the actual evils of Rome, which John's first readers would have no difficulty in perceiving and identifying, and also continually finds new targets in the world as known to subsequent readers. But its original specificity should warn us against a merely generalizing application today. If the book of Revelation is to illuminate our contemporary world, it will not do to talk vaguely and generally about 'human society in opposition to God'. We need to be as specific as John was in discerning the evils of Babylon in today's world. We need political and economic analysis to see them at work. Of course, specific application of Revelation can easily be abused, by those who wish to claim that such-and-such an evil empire is *the* object of John's prophecy, the last human empire of all, whose imminent collapse will be the end of history. That is not how to read apocalyptic prophecy. Specific application can also be abused as an ideological weapon, where the labelling of one's national enemies as evil Babylon serves to demonize them and to foster and sustain antagonism. By contrast, John's prophecy has a rather disturbing feature—which is something of a habit in biblical prophecy. As we shall see, its condemnation of other people—the city of Rome—boomerangs back on the readers—the Christians of the seven churches of Asia—and constitutes a rather painful challenge to them. But before explaining that feature of Revelation 18, it will be useful to illustrate how specific the chapter is in its application to contemporary Rome.

'All your luxuries and your glittering prizes'[8]
The list of cargoes brought to Rome in Revelation 18.12—13 merits careful attention. Its Old Testament precedent is Ezekiel's account of Tyre's trade (Ezek. 27.12—24), but although there are many items in common between the two lists, John's is far from a slavish copy of Ezekiel's. Rather it is an accurate, not exhaustive but very representative, list of the luxury goods which flowed into Rome from all over the known world in John's time. Items not found in Ezekiel's list (such as silk, pearls, marble, citron-wood, fine flour, chariots) are included by John as highly characteristic of Rome's expensive tastes. But as well as the individual items listed, there is another significant difference between Ezekiel's account of Tyre's trade and John's account of Rome's. Tyre was the middleman through whom all the trade passed, and grew rich on the profits of its trade. Rome, on the other hand, was where all the expensive goods John lists ended up. Rome was their consumer. It did not need to be said that Rome grew rich from the plundering and taxation of her provinces. It was the wealth of her subjects she squandered on the extravagant luxuries listed in these verses. This is one sense, among others, in which Babylon, the high-spending harlot, rode on the back of the beast, the military conqueror.

Aelius Aristides, who wrote a euology of Rome in the middle of the second century, described how merchandise from every part of the known world poured into Rome, so that, if someone should wish to view all these things, he must either see them by travelling over the whole world or be in this city . . . So many merchant ships arrive here, conveying every kind of goods from every people every hour and every day, so that the city is like a factory common to the whole earth . . . So everything comes together here, trade, seafaring, farming, the scourings of the mines, all crafts that exist or have existed, all that is produced and grown. Whatever one does not see here, is not a thing which has existed or exists.[9]

The point is well illustrated by John's list: silver from Spain, citron-wood from Morocco, wheat and fine linen from Egypt, purple from Phoenicia, horses from Greece, frankincense from southern Arabia, ivory, spices, perfumes and jewels from India, silk and cinnamon from China. The sheer distance which silk, for example, had to travel to reach Rome made it as expensive as gold. Almost all the items in the list are luxury items, catering for the vulgar opulence of the Roman upper classes of this period.

The exploitation of the provinces had given the upper classes of Rome excess wealth which they were constantly in search of ways of spending in conspicuous and often outrageous ways. Some of the items of the list (in order) can illustrate the point.[10] The use of solid gold vessels for meals actually had to be forbidden by law, in one of the periodic attempts to curb extravagance, but eating off silver dishes was commonplace, and wealthy ladies would bathe only in silver baths. Pearls of vast expense were not only worn as jewels, but set before guests at banquets, to be dissolved in wine and drunk—for the sake of the thrill of swallowing something of so much value. The aromatic citron-wood was used especially for table-tops, and since the trees only rarely grow large enough to provide table-tops, tables made of this wood were extremely expensive. Nero's prime minister Seneca had three hundred such tables with marble legs. Ivory was so much used for ostentatious decoration that the satirist Juvenal complained that 'nowadays a rich man takes no pleasure in his dinner—his turbot and venison have no taste, his unguents and his roses seem to smell rotten—unless the broad slabs of his dinner table rest upon a rampant, gaping leopard of solid ivory'. Marble, not used for building purposes in Rome until the Empire, came to be so widely used that the Emperor Augustus could boast that he found Rome brick and left it marble. The chariots, often silver-plated, were the horse-drawn four-wheeled private chariots in which wealthy Romans drove around the city.

'Fine flour' was imported for the rich, but wheat, of course, was a staple, not a luxury, food. Nevertheless, the vast cargoes of wheat which Rome imported from Egypt make their own point about the way in which Rome drained the resources of the Empire into itself. Rome could support its rapidly expanding population only by providing monthly hand-outs of corn at government expense—half of the famous 'bread and circuses'[11] with which Rome kept its populace happy.[12] But of course this was not providing for the poor at the expense of the rich; it was providing for the poor of Rome at the expense of the poor in the rest of the Empire.

Slaves come at the end of the list, perhaps because for the even moderately affluent they were a necessity, not a luxury, though slaves of special beauty or skill could fetch very high prices. But John undoubtedly intends a climax: the essential inhumanity of Rome's economic exploitation of the Empire reveals itself unambiguously in the constant flow of slaves from the rest of the Empire to the city of Rome. By John's time slaves made up about half of the population of the city.

The last four words in the Greek of verse 13 are, literally, 'bodies and [or that is] souls [or lives] of human beings'. John has put together a common term for slaves—'bodies'—with the phrase used in Ezekiel 27.13: 'human souls'. Perhaps we should follow many of the English translations and render: 'slaves, that is, human lives'. In that case, John is pointing out that slaves are not mere animal carcasses—'bodies' as they were commonly called in the slave markets—to be bought and sold as property, but are human beings. But it is also possible that he meant to say 'slaves *and* human lives'—intending, with the final two words, to refer to something even more sinister than the regular slave trade. For as well as the slaves who were manual and clerical workers in the houses of the great, there were others, along with prisoners of war and convicted criminals, whose fate was to fight for their lives and die for the entertainment of the Roman crowds in the amphitheatres purpose-built by the Caesars. These victims too were among the delicious fruits to which Roman taste had become accustomed (v. 14).

Some commentators see this list as epitomizing 'the beauties and amenities of the civilized world',[13] which John must surely have appreciated, even while he deplored their idolatrous misuse. No doubt the Roman upper classes saw their luxurious lifestyle as a fine achievement of human culture, but it was a mark of their decadence that they did so. John was not so polite, nor need we be. The list of Roman imports represents self-indulgence such as even Roman moralists and satirists condemned, which could be enjoyed only through criminal disregard for the lives and dignity of very large numbers of other human beings. The amphitheatres symbolize the sadistic contempt for human life which by no means simply qualified the grandeur that was Rome, but lay at its foundation.

Those Who Mourn for Her

The commentators just mentioned make their mistake because they unwittingly read the passage from an inappropriate hermeneutical standpoint. It betrays the outlook of people who instinctively feel some admiration for the opulence of Rome and can contemplate its destruction only with regret. But John, who wrote from exile on Patmos, is much more likely to have seen the greatness of Rome through the eyes of those who suffered because of it. Allan Boesak, who reads the Apocalypse from the perspective of those people in a modern society who are excluded from the affluence of its minority ruling class, makes this point about hermeneutical standpoint rather well. He says that the interpretation we have criticized is 'so typically the viewpoint of those who do not know what it means to stand at the bottom of the list'[14]—meaning at the end of John's list of Roman imports, where the slaves stand.

There is a sense in which John deliberately laid a hermeneutical trap into which the commentators in question have fallen. When they say, for example, that 'it is with infinite pathos that John surveys the loss of so much wealth',[15] they do so because they take the laments for Babylon's fall in verses 10, 16—17, 18—19 as expressing a sorrow John shares. But this is to neglect to notice that John attributes these laments to three very definite classes of people: the kings of the earth (v. 9), the merchants of the earth (v. 11), and the ships' captains and sailors (v. 17). These are precisely the people who themselves benefited from Rome's economic exploitation of the Empire. What they lament is the destruction of the source of their own wealth.

The 'kings of the earth', whom John consistently brands as

those 'who have committed fornication with' the harlot (17.2; 18.3, 9), are not just the client kings who put their own kingdoms under the umbrella of the Roman Empire, but more generally the local ruling classes who throughout the Empire Rome co-opted to a share in her own rule. For them Roman authority served to prop up their own dominant position in their society. Naturally, therefore, it is the destruction of Rome's *power* which they lament (18.10). But, of course, the power they shared with Rome had its economic advantages.[16]

As for the merchants, who 'gained wealth from her' (v. 15), they 'were the great men of the earth' (v. 23). The following statement by a great modern historian of the Roman Empire, himself rather an admirer of its economic development, is perhaps the best comment:

> Capitalistic methods were more successful in trade than in any other department of economic activity during the empire. The merchants, together with the great landowners, were the richest men of the time. They formed important trading companies and associations. The merchants interested in shipping, called *naucleri* or *navicularii*, combined in companies of this kind, and became one of the most powerful economic alliances in the empire.[17]

The point of this last sentence is that, because of the expense and delay of transport by road, it was only trade by shipping that was really profitable. This explains why the third interested party among the mourners for Babylon is the maritime transport industry: 'all who had ships at sea grew rich by her wealth!' (v. 19). All of Rome's imports reached her by sea.[18]

Thus verses 9–19 allow us to see the fall of Rome from a very definite perspective which was certainly not John's: the perspective of those who had grown powerful and rich through their involvement with Rome and her economic system. For such people, of course, Rome's downfall is also their own. No wonder they mourn! The perspective John shares is not that of these people of the *earth* and the *sea* (vv. 9, 11, 17), but that of *heaven* (18.20;[19] 19.1): from this perspective the fall of Babylon is cause for rejoicing and praise of God.

Why then does John give us the perspective of Rome's collaborators in evil: the ruling classes, the mercantile magnates, the shipping industry? I have suggested that he was setting a kind of hermeneutical trap. Any reader who finds himself sharing that perspective—viewing the prospect of the fall of Rome with dismay—should thereby discover, with a shock, where he stands, and the peril in which he stands. And for such readers, it is of the utmost significance that, prior to the picture of the mourners, comes the command:

> Come out of her, my people,
> lest you take part in her sins,
> lest you share in her plagues (v. 4, RSV).

The command, whose language is borrowed from Jeremiah 51.45 (cf. Jer. 50.8; 51.6, 9; Isa. 48.20), is not meant in the literal geographical sense it had in Jeremiah. None of John's first readers lived in the city of Rome. The command is for the readers to *dissociate* themselves from Rome's evil, lest they share her guilt and her judgement. It is a command not to be in the company of those who are then depicted mourning for Babylon.

Revelation's first readers, as we know from the seven messages to the churches in chapters 2—3, were by no means all poor and persecuted like the Christians at Smyrna. Many were affluent, self-satisfied and *compromising*, and for them John intended an urgent revelation of the requirements and the peril of their situation. Most of the seven cities of Asia were prosperous communities with significant stakes, as ports or as commercial, administrative and religious centres, in Roman rule and Roman commerce.[20] But in order to participate in the business and social life of these cities, and so in the prosperity of their wealthier citizens, Christians had to participate also in idolatrous religion, including the Roman state religion. The Nicolaitans, apparently active in several of the churches (2.6, 15), and the prophetess Jezebel at Thyatira, were evidently advocating that such compromise was quite permissible (2.14, 20).[21]

We should note, as the Christians at Thyatira would certainly have noticed, the resemblance between Jezebel, as John portrays her in the message to Thyatira, and the harlot Babylon, as he portrays her in chapters 17—18. Of course, Jezebel is John's symbolic name for the prophetess, just as Babylon is his symbolic name for Rome. It serves to compare her with the Old Testament queen who seduced Israel into idolatry in the time of Elijah. Once reminded of the Old Testament Jezebel's 'harlotries and sorceries' (2 Kings 9.22) and her slaughter of the prophets of the Lord

(1 Kings 18.13), we can see that the harlot of Babylon is also in part modelled on Jezebel (cf. 18.7, 23, 24). Thus it appears that the Thyatiran prophetess, who was encouraging her followers to participate without qualms of conscience in the thriving commercial life of the city, was, so to speak, the local representative of the harlot of Babylon within the church at Thyatira. Through her the seductive power of Rome's alliance of commerce and idolatrous religion was penetrating the church. Some of her followers—who have 'committed adultery with' her (2.22)—might therefore find themselves, with a salutary shock of recognition, among 'the merchants of the earth [who] have grown rich with the wealth of [Babylon's] wantonness' (18.3). Thus John's prophecy against Rome could also become a painful and demanding challenge to some of his Christian readers, who needed to 'come out of her'.

A City Drunk with Blood

The portrait of the harlot in Revelation 17.1—6 ends with a fresh and more sinister use of the image of drunkenness: she who made the earth drunk with her seductive wiles is herself 'drunk with the blood of the saints and the blood of the witnesses of Jesus' (17.6). The accusation recurs, this time with a judicial image, in 18.24. Chapter 18 has announced God's judgement on Babylon for her corruption of the earth (18.3), her luxury and pride (18.7), and central to the chapter, as we have seen, is her economic exploitation. But the climax, and the clinching evidence against her, comes in verse 24: 'in her was found the blood of prophets and of saints, and of all who have been slain on earth'.

The prophets and saints are the Christian martyrs, and many commentators understand 'all who have been slain on earth' also as Christian martyrs, but this is not the natural sense, and it robs the verse of its climax. Rome is indicted not only for the martyrdom of Christians, but also for the slaughter of all the innocent victims of its murderous policies.[22] John has not forgotten that Babylon rides on the beast with its bear's hug and its lion's teeth (13.2). He knows that the *Pax Romana* was, in Tacitus's phrase, 'peace with bloodshed',[23] established by violent conquest, maintained by continual war on the frontiers, and requiring repression of dissent.[24] He knows the connection between Rome's affluence, Rome's idolatrous self-deification, and Rome's military and political brutality. Like every society which absolutizes its own power and prosperity, the Roman Empire could not exist without victims.

What is remarkable about verse 24 is the sense of solidarity it voices between the Christian martyrs and all the other innocent victims of Rome. If John urges his churches to dissociate themselves from the political and economic power-structures of Rome, this is not to turn them into an inward-looking sectarian group, concerned only with their own fate. It is rather because, in their prophetic witness to the world, these followers of the Lamb, himself a victim of Rome, cannot be allied with the murderers but must witness against the murderers. Inevitably they themselves will be victims. The single name of Antipas of Pergamum (2.13) stands in Revelation representatively for all the anonymous victims of Roman absolutism.

Even more remarkable is the faith of Revelation that the future lies 'not with the violent victors of history, but with their victims'.[25] This was possible only through Christian faith in the victory of the slain Lamb (5.5—6).

Conclusions for Today

Those who imagine early Christianity as a quietist and apolitical movement should study the book of Revelation. So should those who suppose that the early Church found nothing to criticize in Roman rule except the imperial cult. In Revelation's exposure of the evil of Rome, the worship of the Emperor and the consequent persecution of the Church are not an isolated aberration, but follow from the fundamental nature of the Roman Empire: Rome's single-minded pursuit of her own power and economic advantage. When the followers of Jesus refused the act of religious loyalty to the Emperor required by the state religion, they were not only denying to Caesar the unconditional loyalty that belonged only to the truly divine King. They witnessed also to a different kind of rule from Caesar's, a Kingdom founded not on exploitative power but on sacrificial service.

In view of the prominence of the economic theme in Revelation 18, it is hard to avoid seeing a modern parallel in the economic relations between the so-called First and Third Worlds. It is easy, from our cultural distance, to recognize the decadence of a culture in which party guests were served with pearls dissolved in wine—thousands of pounds consumed in a few mouthfuls. But the affluent West of today has equally absurd forms of extravagant consumption. Of course, the *way* in which Rome fed her own luxurious tastes by plundering and taxing her Empire is not paralleled in our post-colonial world, and this must warn us against any simplistic transference of judgement from the one case to the other. The First World's contemporary exploitation of the Third takes different forms, which have to be exposed by serious economic analysis before they can be condemned and countered. But there is much to suggest that modern Western society, in its worship of the idol of its own ever-increasing material prosperity,[26] is trafficking in human lives. Chief among its mourners may be the multinational companies, the advertising industry, and the arms trade. But we should also beware the hermeneutical trap John laid for us all.

7: Exodus and Service

Freedom in the Bible

So far in this book we have engaged in detailed exegesis of particular passages of Scripture, while setting them in the context of the whole of Scripture. This kind of detailed attention to particular passages is essential to a proper understanding of biblical teaching on any topic. But equally important is the attempt to trace the broad contours of a particular theme in the Bible as a whole. The Bible is a collection of very different types of writings written over a very long period by a large number of authors and editors. So in the nature of the case we cannot expect it to provide us with ready-made summaries of its own teaching in all its component parts—though there are a few statements which come close to this (e.g. Matt. 22.37—40). For the most part, the task of discerning the general thrust and major components of the Bible's treatment of a topic is a difficult task of creative interpretation. It requires much more than the gathering of relevant information from all parts of Scripture. The appropriate categories for a synthesis may not be handed to the interpreter on a plate by Scripture itself: he may need to search for the most appropriate categories or to invent new ones. Without discounting any part of the scriptural witness, judgements will have to be made about what is central and what is peripheral, what is relative and what is absolute, or what is provisional and what is enduring. In some cases it will be important not only to report the actual positions reached by particular biblical writings, but to discern the direction in which biblical thinking is moving. For the Bible contains the records of a dynamic, developing tradition of thought, and the aim of interpretation should be to let Scripture involve its readers in its own process of thought, so that their own thinking may continue in the direction it sets. In this chapter, we shall attempt an example of this task of synthesizing biblical teaching on a topic by examining the theme of freedom in the Bible.

Introduction

'The bigger the words, the more easily alien elements are able to hide in them. This is particularly the case with freedom,' observed Ernst Bloch.[1] Because freedom is such a 'big' word, appealing to such fundamental human aspirations and therefore so politically potent, it is easily abused. The defence or promotion of one form of freedom is frequently used as a political excuse for suppressing other forms of freedom. As often as the word seems to open unlimited horizons of human self-fulfilment for those who aspire to freedom, so often its real meaning is reduced to a minimum by those who use it to acquire or maintain political power. Because all too often the selective use of the Bible has been used to justify the restriction of freedom—in the claim that the Bible endorses only *this* kind of freedom and *not that*—we must try to be open to the actual dimensions of freedom in Scripture. And because the ambiguity of the notion of freedom makes it all too easy to cloak our own concept in biblical rhetoric, we need to work hard at discerning the central thrust of the Bible's understanding of freedom.

We are not looking in the Bible for some kind of blueprint for a free society today. Just as forms of human society have necessarily changed and developed—especially in complexity—since biblical times, so political liberties have developed and continue to develop. Specific freedoms which need to be embodied and safeguarded politically are historical in character, however much they may be rooted in fundamental human nature. We cannot expect to find them ready-made in Scripture, which can tell us nothing directly about, for example, the freedom of the press or even freedom of religious worship. What we are looking for is the direction in which the Bible points, the fundamental nature of God's will for human freedom. This is what we need in order to follow that direction into the dimensions of liberation which are required in our contemporary world.

Relevant material in the Bible is plentiful, but will not be found merely or even mainly by looking for the word 'freedom', which the Old Testament almost never uses and which is not at all common in the New Testament, or for related words which are rather more common but still do not indicate the scope of the theme.[2] The notion of freedom is much more central to the biblical message than words alone would suggest. For example, the Exodus, which throughout both testaments is frequently recalled as an event and used as a model or metaphor for later events and experiences, always carried powerful connotations of liberation from oppression.[3] The Old Testament constantly identifies God, from this event, as 'the Lord your God, who brought you out of . . . the house of bondage' (Exod. 20.2 etc.). 'This is the Old Testament definition of God: God the liberator.'[4] A somewhat similar significance attaches to the fact that, in Luke's Gospel, Jesus' mission is programmatically described at the outset of his ministry as a mission of liberation: 'To proclaim release to the captives . . . to set at liberty those who are oppressed' (Luke 4.18). We can expect the theme of freedom to encompass rather a large area of biblical concerns.

God's Freed Slaves

The Old Testament has no abstract definition of freedom, but conceives of freedom in quite concrete terms. Obviously, enslavement means subjection to the will of another, and freedom is therefore freedom from constraint or coercion. But in the paradigmatic case of Israel's enslavement in Egypt, for example, it is not the abstract status of subjection but the concrete evils of oppression—intolerably hard labour, enforced infanticide (Exod. 1.11—16)—which distress the people and evoke God's concern and redemptive action (Exod. 2.23—5; 3.7—10; 6.5—7). This is not to say that Old Testament people did not value freedom in itself, but simply that its value was felt, as it is for most people, in its concrete benefits: freedom to supply one's basic needs and to enjoy the ordinary pleasures of life without being exploited by others.

Consequently, to exchange the lordship of the Egyptians for the lordship of God was not to move from one slavery to another, since God was dedicated to the interests of his people and his lordship was experienced as liberation from all human lordship. From her sense of being a nation of freed slaves, with only a divine master, Israel acquired an unusual (in the ancient Near Eastern context) sense of the equal right to freedom of all Israelites. The principle which Leviticus 25.42 expresses with reference to the actual institution of slavery militated against all relationships of subjection among Israelites: 'they are *my* slaves, whom I brought out of the land of Egypt; they shall not be sold as slaves'. A similar consideration is at work in 1 Samuel 8, in which the people are foolishly not content with having God as their king, but want a human king 'like all the nations'. Samuel's argument is that they will be subjecting themselves to the kind of oppressive despotism which much contemporary monarchy amounted to, and his catalogue of the evils of monarchy is summed up: 'you shall be his slaves' (1 Sam. 8.17). A political relationship of subjection was inappropriate in the nation God had redeemed from slavery (see also Judg. 8.22—3).

All over the ancient world (and not only the ancient world) freedom for some meant subjection for others. To be free meant to be a master, and therefore to have slaves. So rulers were free at the expense of their subjects, masters at the expense of their slaves, the rich and powerful at the expense of the poor and vulnerable, men at the expense of women. In Israel this correlation between freedom and subjection was broken through *in principle*, because Israel, and thus all Israelites, had been liberated by God and were his slaves alone. Hence, in Israel, freedom entailed not inequality, but equality. That this *principle* of freedom was not carried through with complete consistency—in relation, for example, to the status of women, or to the institution of slavery (to which we shall return below)—should not obscure the enormous significance of the breakthrough in principle.

Economic Independence
Much of the Old Testament law, and many of the denunciations of the prophets, are concerned with the danger of exploitation (loss of freedom) arising from social and economic inequalities. This not only required impartiality in the administration of laws which enshrined every Israelite's right to freedom from harm to his life and livelihood. It also meant that the law and the prophets were positively concerned with maintaining the economic independence of Israelite families, consisting in their inalienable right to a share in the land which God had given to all Israel. The loss of economic independence made people vulnerable to exploitation by others and would often lead to actual enslavement. Hence the prophets denounced those who accumulated property, 'who add house to house and join field to field, until not an acre remains, and you are left to dwell alone in the land' (Isa. 5.8, NEB). Hence also the constant concern to protect those who did not have economic independence: resident aliens, orphans, widows. No one in Israel, not even resident aliens, should be exploited, since it was precisely from oppression as landless aliens in Egypt that God redeemed Israel (Exod. 23.9; Lev. 19.33—4; Deut. 24.18).

Thus the ideal of freedom in Israel took the concrete forms of economic independence and freedom from fear of harm. This imposed, it should be noticed, not only the kinds of restraints which all legal systems impose—against obvious kinds of harm to the persons and property of others—but also economic restraints, since only a relative equality of economic resources could prevent the effective oppression of the poor by wealthier classes. In practice, social and economic equality was very much eroded during the monarchical period, but this was the burden of many of the prophets' complaints, and the eschatological hope which recurs throughout the prophets expressed the ideal of economic independence and freedom from fear of harm for all: 'they shall sit every man under his vine and under his fig tree, and none shall make them afraid' (Mic. 4.4).[5]

A final observation may be needed to correct any impression that freedom in Israel was understood purely as freedom for the individual (or family) *from* oppression by others. Such an individualistic understanding of freedom is easily projected back from modern times. If we think of freedom as lordship in correlation with subjection, then freedom for all means that each is his own master, and each experiences others only as limits on his freedom, in competition with him. This is modern liberal individualism. That it was not the ancient Israelite's experience of freedom was in part because the Israelite was not his own master, but God's slave. His acknowledgement of the divine lordship gave him responsibilities to his fellow Israelites. Thus, while it is a fundamental feature of the Old Testament law, as it must be of all realistic attempts to safeguard freedom, that it embodies many restraints on anti-social abuse of freedom, it is equally character-istic of Old Testament law that it enjoins positive caring helpfulness for others. My neighbour is not simply a restraint on my freedom, but one whom I am to love as myself (Lev. 19.18). The New Testament's understanding of freedom as not so much *from* others as *for* others is already implicit in the Old Testament sense of social responsibility.

Slavery in the Old Testament
The institution of slavery, of course, existed in Old Testament Israel, and Old Testament law contains a good many laws intended to regulate it.[6] In accordance with common practice in the ancient Near East, slaves were both foreigners, captured as prisoners of war, and Israelites, who had fallen disastrously into debt and had

to sell themselves into slavery. Slavery meant that the master had very considerable rights over his slave and the rights of the slave, though not abolished altogether, were very restricted.

However, it is important to notice, first of all, that the Old Testament fully recognizes the inconsistency of the enslavement of Israelites with the fundamental freedom and equality of all God's people, whom he redeemed from slavery in Egypt. The legislation accepts the fact of slavery but treats it as an abnormality to be minimized as far as possible. It therefore gives slaves the opportunity of release, after six years, without payment for their release (Exod. 21.2), and in fact with provisions to tide them over a period of unemployment (Deut. 15.13−14). Only by free choice could a slave opt, instead of release after six years, for remaining permanently in his master's service (Exod. 21.5−6; Deut. 15.16−17). These laws attempt, in the face of economic realities which produced slavery, to give some continued substance to the fundamental right of Israelites to freedom. It is because 'you were a slave in the land of Egypt, and the LORD your God redeemed you' (Deut. 15.15), that the master is to liberate his slaves after six years of service.

The law in Leviticus 25.39−43 goes further. While allowing Israelites to possess foreign slaves (25.44−6), it prohibits the actual enslavement of fellow Israelites, who may be forced by poverty only into a kind of semi-slave status. This is probably an attempt to deprive the existing practice of slavery of the legal status of slavery, though some scholars have argued that all the other laws on slavery refer only to non-Israelite slaves.[7] In any case, the theological reason given for not enslaving fellow Israelites is noteworthy: 'they are my slaves, whom I brought forth out of the land of Egypt; they shall not be sold as slaves' (19.42).

In addition to recognizing the fundamental right of all Israelites to freedom, some of the laws also have the effect of considerably mitigating and humanizing the institution of slavery, in ways which are not paralleled in other ancient societies. The laws protecting slaves against their own masters (Exod. 21.20−1, 26−7) are unique in their contemporary context, and represent a step beyond the legal treatment of slaves as no more than chattels: as mere property they could have no rights to protection from harm by their owners, but as human beings they do. The laws on release and on runaway slaves (Exod. 21.2−6; Deut. 15.12−18; 23.15−16) must, if effective, have ensured that slavery was not very oppressive in practice, since a harsh master would not have been able to keep his slave. Since an obligation to return runaway slaves to their masters was taken for granted in ancient society (cf. 1 Sam. 30.15), the law commanding Israelites on the contrary to harbour runaway slaves (Deut. 23.15–16) is again quite remarkable. Though the motivation is not stated, Israelites would remember, readily enough, that Israel originated as a nation of runaway slaves. The sympathies of such people should therefore belong with the runaway slave rather than with his master.[8] Thus, while not actually abolishing an institution which was universal in the ancient world, the Old Testament law did considerably humanize and even, we might say, undermine it, as a result of Israel's experience of liberation from Egypt. Even concubines captured in war were human beings with rights to be respected (Deut. 21.10–14).

If the law and the prophets (cf. Jer. 34) based their attitude to slavery on the salvation-historical ground of the Exodus liberation, it is typical of the wisdom literature that it reaches the same conclusion on creation-theological grounds: that the same God created both master and slave (Job 31.13–15). In the end both kinds of argument require the abolition of slavery, and it is perfectly proper that we should follow the *direction* of these Old Testament principles as far as they point, even beyond Old Testament practice and, for that matter, even beyond New Testament practice. Indeed, they carry us further than the abolition of slavery defined in a narrow sense. All relationships of subjection which permit the exploitation of one human being by another are contrary to the fundamental will of God as the Old Testament reveals it. They have no basis in the created status of human beings, who are all equally subject to God, and the historical purpose of God is for the abolition of all such relationships. His liberation of Israel from slavery cannot, in the end, be an exclusive privilege for Israel alone, but is prototypical of his will that all humanity should similarly come under his liberating lordship.

Freedom in the New Testament

The concept of freedom undergoes major development in the New Testament. In attempting to delineate this briefly, we shall focus on four aspects which are relevant to our particular concern with political forms of freedom.

In the first place, the New Testament *deepens and extends* the whole issue of freedom and subjection, taking it into areas beyond the reach of politics and law. Thus Jesus' ministry freed no slaves of men, but liberated slaves of guilt and sin, those held captive by demons, oppressed by disease and handicaps, imprisoned in themselves, and subject to death. The Exodus liberation thus becomes in the New Testament a type of Christ's liberation of those enslaved to sin and death (e.g. Rev. 1.5—6). But this is precisely an extension and deepening of the Old Testament concept of freedom, not a replacement of it. A liberation from all oppression cannot exclude the political sphere, even while it goes much further than the political.

Second, the implications of freedom in Christ certainly affected the social life of the Church, the new people of God liberated by the new Exodus. Christian freedom, in the New Testament, is certainly not purely inward and individual, but concerns the outward, social relationships of Christians in the Church. In principle, there can be no relationships of subjection among Christians, 'neither slave nor free' (Gal. 3.28). Some New Testament advice to masters and slaves could be understood as merely ameliorating the situation, without changing the fundamental relationship, but Philemon 16 carried through the basic Christian principle more consistently. Philemon is to receive back his runaway slave Onesimus '*no longer as a slave*, but more than a slave, as a beloved brother'. The legal form of slavery is retained, but master and slave are to relate no longer as master and slave, but as brothers.

Perhaps even more remarkable is Ephesians 5.21—6.9, which deals with three types of authority-relationship (wives and husbands, children and parents, slaves and masters). Here the asymmetrical advice given to the respective parties in the first two relationships must be balanced by the fact that all three relationships come under the rubric in 5.21, which is fully reciprocal: 'Be subject to one another out of reverence for Christ.' The principle of freedom in mutual service underlies the more socially determined elements of authority in the discussion of family relationships. But lest the point of the rubric had been forgotten by the time the reader reached the third relationship (slaves and masters), it is reiterated there in a quite startling form. When the masters are told to 'do the same' to their slaves (6.9), the reference can only be to rendering service as a slave (6.7). In other words, if the slaves are told to be good slaves to their masters, 'as to the Master' (6.7), the masters are also told *to be slaves* to their slaves, 'as to the Master'. Presumably they are to exercise their authority in a way which is just as much a service to their slaves as the slaves' work is service to them. Such advice taken seriously would mean that the continuing outward order of freedom and subjection would be inwardly transformed by the new Christian principle of freedom in mutual service (see the fourth point below). It should also be noticed that the way the master—slave relationship is here transcended is not by making everyone masters, but by making everyone slaves: this leads to our next point.

Third, the New Testament gives a quite new emphasis to freedom as voluntary service. Although the New Testament continues to use the somewhat paradoxical language which equates subjection to God's lordship with freedom (e.g. 1 Pet. 2.16), the heart of its understanding of freedom is that, through Jesus the Son of God, Christians are free *sons and daughters* of God their Father (John 8.32; Gal. 4.7; Rom. 8.14—17). The point is that, while a son fulfils himself in dedicated obedience to his father's will, as Jesus did, this is not the involuntary subjection of a slave, but the glad and willing service of a son. Voluntary service to God means also, again on the model of Jesus, voluntary service of others. Instead of replacing a model of society in which there are masters and slaves with a model in which everyone is his own master, Jesus and the early Church replaced it with a model in which everyone is the slave of others—with, of course, the understanding that this 'slavery' is entirely willing (Luke 22.26—7; John 13.14; Gal. 5.13). In other words, freedom is the freedom to love: 'you were called to freedom, brothers and sisters; only do not use this freedom for the advantage of the flesh [i.e. selfishly], but through love serve one another as slaves' (Gal. 5.13).[9] If the Old Testament emphasis is on God's people as *freed* slaves, the New Testament emphasis is on God's people as *free* slaves.

Authority in the Church is no exception to this principle. It exists only in the form of service ('ourselves as your slaves for Jesus' sake', 2 Cor. 4.5, RSV, mg.; cf. Mark 10.43—4; Matt. 23.10—11), and therefore as part of a pattern of mutual submission and service by all to all.[10] Hence freedom in this form, as the spirit of glad and loving service, creates not a collection of independent and competitive individuals, but a real *community* of mutual dependence. Exploitative relationships are replaced by liberating relationships.

Fourth, this to some extent explains the early Church's attitude to the existing structures of political and social subjection in their contemporary society. They did not attempt to abolish them in the name of freedom, but they did attempt to transform them from within by turning them into relationships of *voluntary* and (where possible) *mutual* subjection. This is most evident in Ephesians 5.21–6.9, with regard to marriage, parenthood and slavery, as we have already noticed, and in 1 Peter 2.13–17, with regard to political structures. In this last case, while government remained wholly outside the Church's influence, it could not enjoin *mutual* subjection, but Christians' acknowledgement of the authority of the state is notably linked with the freedom of God's slaves (v. 16).

Arguably, this strategy of Christian transformation of authoritarian structures from within was both more practicable than and, in its own way, as effective as any attempt to set up new egalitarian structures. In the end, egalitarian structures are also required, but in themselves they cannot produce freedom in its fullest sense. They may be vehicles for the competitive liberty which is still enslaved to self-service, rather than the true freedom which creates community.

Concepts of Freedom

All too often in church history God has been misrepresented as suppressing rather than promoting freedom. He has been the heavenly despot who is the model and sanction for oppressive regimes on earth: divine right monarchies in the state, clerical rule in the Church, patriarchal domination in the family. It is clear that this is not the biblical God. His lordship liberates from all human lordship. His slaves may not be slaves of any human master (Lev. 25.42). Those who call God their Father and Christ their Master may call no man either (Matt. 23.9–10). This is because the divine Master himself fulfils his lordship not in domination but in the service of a slave (Phil. 2.6–11).

But what kind of freedom is it that the biblical God promotes? According to liberal individualism, which is still highly influential in Western democracies, 'the only freedom which deserves the name, is that of pursuing our own good in our own way, so long as we do not attempt to deprive others of theirs, or impede their efforts to attain it' (John Stuart Mill).[11] Perhaps a definition of the biblical understanding of freedom might be formulated in parallel to Mill's definition: the only freedom which deserves the name is that of freely pursuing the good of others, not by depriving them of liberty but by promoting their liberty. Mill's definition creates a tension between freedom, so defined, and equality. The state's positive activities towards the common good seem to conflict with the individual's liberty to pursue his own good. The tension between individual freedom and social justice pervades contemporary British politics as perceived by the politicians and many others. For example, a kind of freedom which government attempts to maximize is freedom of consumer choice, but this is a kind of freedom which too easily benefits the affluent at the expense of the inability of the poor to choose anything other than poverty.

Our definition of freedom, according to which the individual is most free, not in self-fulfilment for his or her own sake, but in self-giving for others, escapes the tension between freedom and social justice, but, as soon as it is applied to the political sphere, creates a different tension: between freedom and coercion. Government is characteristically, though by no means exclusively, the exercise of coercive authority, and even in a democracy that means coercing people to contribute to the common good. Of course, the good citizen, the truly free man in our sense, will welcome the laws which, for example, oblige him to pay taxes to support the welfare state, and he will gladly and willingly obey them. But the unwilling taxpayer is not, as Jean-Jacques Rousseau maintained, being 'forced to be free': he is simply not, in this respect, free. If Rousseau were right, a totalitarian state would be the political structure most closely corresponding to our definition of freedom. But he is wrong, because it is a contradiction in terms to think that freedom can be created by coercion. This being so, a democratic system provides the only adequate structural context for freedom in the political sphere. It reduces the tension between freedom and coercion as far as possible, but the tension remains. Political education, within a democratic system, reduces it somewhat further, but cannot eliminate it.

It becomes evident, as so often when we relate the New Testament to politics, that the political sphere, important as it is, is neither all-embracing nor self-sufficient. The freedom which creates a real and healthy political community can only to a limited extent be created by political means. It arises from those deeper dimensions of enslavement and liberty to which Jesus' liberating mission was directed.

113

The Dimensions of Freedom

Freedom in the Bible is a broad and complex notion. It extends, for example, from the freedom from Egyptian oppression which the Israelites were given at the Exodus to the freedom of Jesus' acceptance of suffering and death out of love for humanity and faithfulness to his Father's will. It embraces freedoms *from* (exploitation, for example), freedoms *of* (choice, for example), freedoms *for* (service of others, for example), freedoms *to* (hope, for example). It is as complex as human life, and no one model can adequately categorize it. But a model which can help to counter the frequent tendency to reduce freedom to certain types of freedom is that of *multidimensional* freedom corresponding to a multi-dimensional model of human life and experience.[12]

Human life can be understood as having a variety of dimensions: such as the psychological, the physical (relating to the body), the immediate social (person-to-person relations), the economic, the cultural, the political, the technological, the environmental (human society's relation to nature). Any such list of dimensions is flexible: others could be added and distinctions made in different ways, because these are not absolute distinctions inherent in human experience, but convenient categories for thinking about a complex whole. The dimensions are distinguishable but *interrelated*. Action or experience in one dimension has effects in others. Unemployment, for example, which belongs most obviously in the economic dimension, has drastic psychological and social effects, may make people physically ill, and calls for political action. We should resist attempts to see one dimension as uniquely determinative of the others: as though, for example, economic conditions *determine* (as distinct from merely affecting) all the other dimensions. No one dimension determines unilaterally all the others. Rather the dimensions interrelate in very varied and complex ways.

The political dimension — meaning the ordering of human life for and by government — is one dimension, not, as totalitarian claims would have it, the all-encompassing dimension which includes all the others, but one dimension which can *affect* all the others and in turn be affected by them. The religious dimension can in one sense — as the sphere of specifically religious activities — be treated as another of the many dimensions, but, as the dimension of relationship to God, is more adequately understood as the one *really* all-encompassing dimension. God is the Creator,

Lord and Saviour of human life in all of its dimensions. To know God is to relate to him in all dimensions of life.

Multidimensional thinking enables us to think more flexibly about freedom and liberation. It is not simply that enslavement and oppression occur in many different dimensions of life—economic exploitation, psychological oppression, and so on. It is also that most forms of oppression affect several dimensions and can be attacked by liberating activity in more than one dimension. Thus, for example, physical handicap looks like a problem in one dimension (the physical) which should be tackled in that dimension. If we cannot remove the handicap itself, we might think liberation from the handicap impossible. But in fact the physical handicap in itself may be the least of the handicapped person's problems, since it is compounded by the attitudes of people who treat the handicapped as another species and by the organization of society and the design of buildings, which exclude the handicapped from much of normal society. Freedom for the handicapped can be achieved through action in these other dimensions of the matter, as also, of course, through a kind of psychological liberation in the handicapped person's own attitude to his situation.

With this perspective it is useful to look again at the early Church's treatment of slavery. This was a form of oppression affecting virtually every dimension of life for both slaves and their masters. It could have been abolished as an institution only by strong political action accompanied by radical restructuring of society and the economy and requiring widespread public support. Because early Christians could not and did not attempt this, they could be accused of tolerating slavery. But what they really did was to promote liberation from slavery in *those dimensions* where it was possible: in the psychological and immediate social dimensions. Even the slaves of pagan masters found a kind of liberation from the psychological dehumanization of the slave condition: they recovered the dignity of human equality in a community where they were treated as Christian brothers and sisters. This was not everything, but it was worth having. Where the Church failed was in remaining content with this at a later period, when it gained both the political influence and the power to mould public opinion which would have made the abolition of slavery as an institution at least something which should have been attempted. At this point—and until the nineteenth century—the Church called an artificial halt to the biblical dynamic of freedom which belongs not to one dimension but flows through all.[13] Liberation from slavery within the sphere of the Church's own social relationships could have been the yeast which eventually leavened the whole lump.

The interrelation between the dimensions of freedom is most frequently posed in terms of the relation between inner and outer freedom, or 'spiritual' and 'secular' freedom, or existential and structural freedom.[14] These pairs are not stable or easily delimited, but it is possible to distinguish broadly between, on the one hand, the economic, political and social structures of freedom, and, on the other hand, the kind of personal freedom which is possible even *despite* oppressive structures.[15] That the latter kind of freedom is real and important can be seen, for example, in such extreme cases as Soviet dissidents in the Gulag, remaining free, in their thinking, of the system which oppresses them unbearably, or in the Christian martyrs under the Roman Empire, who could be regarded as the most truly free people of their time, in their refusal to let even the threat of death cow them into submission. Such freedom in and despite oppressive structures is not only real but essential to the cause of liberation *from* oppressive structures. It is only out of their inner liberation from the system that Russian dissidents can publicly protest against and hope to change the system. It needed a Moses liberated by God from resignation to the irresistible power of Pharaoh to lead the people out of Egypt, and it needed the gradual psychological liberation of the people themselves to free them from Egypt even after their escape from Pharaoh's army.

The point is that real freedom cannot be confined to one dimension. Inner freedom cannot rest content with outer unfreedom, though it may have to suffer the contradiction in circumstances where outer freedom is unattainable. Where the experience of existential freedom happily coexists with structural oppression, merely compensating for it rather than reacting against it, it is to that extent inauthentic. Admittedly, one should not press the point where, for example, the churches of the oppressed make life bearable in otherwise unbearable circumstances. African Independent churches in South Africa, for example, provide liberation from the psychological and physical ills of life under apartheid, even if they do remain notoriously apolitical. They are not to be blamed in the way that oppressors who promote purely 'spiritual' versions of Christian freedom for those they oppress must be condemned for abusing the gospel. But the more impressive example is that of American black slaves, who while experiencing the liberation of the gospel, which gave them inner freedom from the dehumanizing effects of enslavement ('I'm a chile of God wid my soul set free / For Christ hab bought my liberty'), were certainly not reconciled to their chains. On the contrary, their experience of the liberating God sustained a longing for outward freedom ('My Lord delivered Daniel / Why can't he deliver me?') which was both eschatological ('Children, we shall be free / When the Lord shall appear') and realistic ('Pharaoh's army got drownded / Oh Mary, don't you weep').[16]

The contribution of the New Testament's insights into the nature of real freedom as liberation from enslavement to self-interest and freedom to give oneself for others is also important in this context. The oppressed who long for freedom are not truly liberated from the system which oppresses them so long as the freedom they desire is only the freedom their oppressors have: freedom for themselves, no matter what this entails for others. In such circumstances the struggle for liberation is simply a mirror-image of the system it opposes: it becomes ruthless in its self-interest, creates as many victims as it liberates, and produces a new kind of tyranny in place of the old. Outward liberation worthy of the name requires people who have been freed to live for others, and for all others, even for their oppressors.[17]

8: The Book of Esther and the Jewish Holocaust

In this chapter and the next we shall be finding modern political relevance in unexpected places in the Old Testament. They illustrate the way in which such relevance can emerge when biblical texts are re-read in the light of new situations. Both are rather striking instances of the way in which parts of the Bible, which, for (in these cases) virtually the whole of Christian history, have seemed of marginal significance to contemporary concerns, can suddenly come into their own in new circumstances.

The book of Esther has offended many Christian readers, at least since Luther, whose oft-quoted remark is not really representative of his own view of Esther but is not untypical of many later critics: 'I am so hostile to this book [2 Maccabees] and to Esther that I could wish they did not exist at all; for they judaize too greatly and have much pagan impropriety.'[1] B. W. Anderson summarizes many subsequent complaints when he writes of

> the discordant note which the book strikes in the ears of those accustomed to hearing the Christian gospel. It is an emphatically Jewish book whose primary purpose is the authorization and regulation of a purely Jewish festival, Purim. In no passage is there unambiguous reference to God . . . Not least of all, the book is inspired by a fierce nationalism and an unblushing vindictiveness which stand in glaring contradiction to the Sermon on the Mount. Surely this book is of the earth, earthy. As we turn to it from other books of the Bible, 'we fall, as it were, from heaven to earth,' as Ewald once remarked.[2]

We shall be taking up these critical reactions to Esther in what follows. To some extent, as we shall see, the modern political relevance of Esther emerges only when the cause of its offensiveness is found to lie as much in ourselves as in the text.

The problem of the historicity of Esther is of no great importance for our purposes. I incline to the view that it belongs somewhere on the spectrum between history and the historical novel. In other words, some real events,[3] now irrecoverable, have been written up with much less concern to report facts than to tell a story effectively. Indeed, the narrative art of the book is grudgingly admired by its worst enemies. However much the plot may be fictional, the truth of the book lies in its insight into a historical situation, conveyed in the way the plot is constructed and the story told.

The Final Solution

It will be as well to start with the modern context to which any responsible contemporary reading of Esther must relate. Many of the objections to the book lose their force when we allow our understanding of it to be illuminated by that event of modern history whose relevance to its theme should be glaringly obvious: the terrible climax of the history of anti-Semitism in the death of six million Jews in the Holocaust. Here we scarcely even have to speak of the new meaning which Esther gains in interaction with this context. Rather, initially at least, we can be content with the way this context serves to highlight the core of the book's original meaning. Beneath its entertaining surface and within the apparatus of a tale of intrigue at an oriental court, Esther is the story of a political attempt to exterminate the Jewish people. The real political issue in Esther is not vindictive nationalism, but the survival of the Jewish nation in the face of the threats posed by anti-Semitism. Although most commentators recognize this theme, it is astonishing how little *attention* it receives even in post-war discussion of the book.

Esther is a story of politics in the Persian Empire, and so its setting is the harem and the court, and its typical scene is the banquet. The tone of this court is already set in the sharply ironic account of the deposition of queen Vashti in chapter 1.[4] Such politics are determined by the rivalries, the passions, the wounded pride, the grudges of courtiers like Haman, who struggle for position and power and manipulate the theoretically absolute power of the Great King. They are redeemed at all only by the loyalty and honesty of courtiers like Mordecai. The issue of the book—the survival of the Jewish people—emerges in this context. It is Mordecai's proud Jewish refusal to perform the customary obeisance before the grand vizier Haman, the enemy of his people, which provokes Haman's attempt at genocide. This monstrously disproportionate response to one man's act of insubordination is explained by the vizier's monstrously inflated self-importance: 'he scorned to lay hands on [Mordecai] alone' (3.6, NEB). But there is more to it than that. In Haman's attempt to implement his revenge the machinations of the court have to take the realities of the Empire into account, and the full weight of anti-Semitism comes into play.

In Haman's advice to the king (3.8), the Jews supposedly pose a *political* problem which can be solved only by their complete elimination. The problem arises from the fact of the Jewish diaspora and the determination of Jews resident in all parts of the Empire to preserve their racial and cultural identity. In Moore's rather apt translation of 3.8, they are 'scattered, yet unassimilated',[5] or as the NEB has it: 'There is a certain people, dispersed among the many peoples in all the provinces of your kingdom, who keep themselves apart.' The suggestion is of an alien element, whose exclusivism is represented as sinister and perhaps subversive. Haman is only drawing the political consequence from a popular dislike and suspicion of the Jews, whose rigorous adherence to the customs prescribed in the law of Moses severely restricted their social contact with Gentiles and set them apart. The familiar cultural and racial dynamics of a situation where a group emphasizes its distinct identity in order to preserve it and thereby incurs the hostility and suspicion of the majority population were already at work at this early stage of the Jewish diaspora. 'Their laws are different from those of every other people', Haman continues (NEB). Many ethnic groups in the vast Persian Empire preserved their distinctive customs and the Empire prided itself on its tolerance of cultural diversity. But in this case, Haman insinuates, their laws conflict with those of the Empire: 'they do not keep your majesty's laws'. He is, of course, generalizing from Mordecai's refusal to honour him, explicitly because Mordecai was a Jew (3.4), but the generalization gains its plausibility from the separateness of the Jews and their absolute, religious loyalty to their own laws. The picture emerges of a subversive, underground movement with its cells in all provinces of the Empire. Therefore, 'it does not benefit your majesty to tolerate them' (NEB).[6]

Haman does not *identify* the people in question to the king, and the king does not inquire who they are. He is content to trust his vizier implicitly, or at least to be swayed by his lavish baksheesh (3.9). So no specifically anti-Semitic prejudice on Xerxes' part is presupposed. But widespread anti-Semitism throughout the

Empire *is* presupposed in Haman's edict (3.13). The genocide it commands requires a body of popular opinion willing to execute it. The fact that Esther had prudently concealed her Jewishness (2.10) also reveals the general atmosphere of anti-Semitism which gives the issue of the book—the survival of the Jewish people—its point. As in so many subsequent pogroms, malicious but plausible political argument is able to exploit popular anti-Semitic attitudes.

Haman's plan, however, is no ordinary pogrom, but a genuine 'final solution' to the 'Jewish problem'. The laborious official language of the edict (3.13, NEB: 'to destroy, slay, and exterminate all Jews, young and old, women and children, in one day') spells out with emphasis the intention which was in any case already clear (3.6, 9) and is more than once re-emphasized as the story continues (4.13; 7.4). The reader is well aware, from the opening verse of the book, that Xerxes' Empire stretched 'from India to Ethiopia'. Virtually all Jews in the world came within the scope of Xerxes' power and Haman's plot. It is not without significance that hardly at any other time in history than during the Persian Empire could a political project to annihilate the whole Jewish race at one blow have been envisaged. If Haman's project is not, in this extreme form, a fact of ancient history, then the author has seized the opportunity of this historical setting to demonstrate imaginatively the scale of the threat posed to his people by the anti-Semitism of their environment. After Auschwitz we can scarcely say he was wrong.

Hitler provides a curious parallel even to the personal source of Haman's plot: Haman's sense of injury to his dignity when the Jew Mordecai refuses to flatter his self-importance and his consequent quest for revenge. In a speech in 1939 Hitler said:

> In the course of my life I have very often been a prophet, and have usually been ridiculed for it. During the time of my struggle for power it was in the first instance the Jewish race which only received my prophecies with laughter when I said that I would one day take over the leadership of the State, and with it that of the whole nation, and that I would then among many other things settle the Jewish problem. Their laughter was uproarious, but I think that for some time now they have been laughing on the other side of their face.[7]

One should not exaggerate the extent to which Haman prefigures Hitler. His motives for the elimination of the Jews were exclusively personal, not (like Hitler's) part of a grand political design. But within the realistic confines of court politics in ancient Persia, he foreshadows the peculiarly twentieth-century politics of the Third Reich. Moreover, there is a sense in which, without deliberately giving Haman a prophetic significance, the author did intend him to transcend the story. Haman is 'the Agagite' (3.1; 8.3; 9.24), which links him with the royal house of the Amalekites (Num. 24.7; 1 Sam. 15.8—9, 32—3), the ancient sworn enemy of Israel (Exod. 17.8—16; Deut. 25.17—19; 1 Sam. 15; 1 Chron. 4.43). It is quite improbable that Haman could have been descended from the Amalekite king Agag, and the term 'Agagite' may originally have had some Persian significance. But in the story the association of Haman with Agag serves to give him a typical significance,[8] which is confirmed by the fact that his enemy Mordecai is a Benjaminite descended from Kish (2.5), like King Saul (1 Sam. 9.1—2), who once defeated Agag in battle (1 Sam. 15). As 'the Agagite' Haman becomes the prototypical enemy of the Jews, and can also be called simply 'the enemy of the Jews' (3.10; 8.1; 9.10; cf. 7.6) or 'the enemy of all the Jews' (9.24). As prototypical, Haman becomes both a *role* which future enemies of the Jews can play and, strung up on the prodigiously high gallows he built for Mordecai, a prophecy of their end. 'Countless generations have recognized [the book of Esther's] story as their own, and gained hope, in sombre moments of history, that the Hamans they knew would be brought low,' wrote Abraham Cohen,[9] referring, of course, to generations of *Jews*.

Not that Christians have never seen Haman as a type of the tyrants who have persecuted the Church. But Esther is peculiarly a story about *Jewish* survival, as the typically anti-Semitic argument of 3.8 makes clear. While it would not be wrong to draw some analogies with other forms of attempted genocide or with persecution of the New Testament people of God, still Christian readers of Esther should be careful not to evade the central issue of the book: the survival of the Jewish people in the face of the threat posed by anti-Semitism. We shall return to this issue after considering another aspect of Esther which also has broader implications.

Politics Without Divine Direction

As well as the charge of vindictive nationalism, another feature of Esther which is often held against it is its allegedly non-religious character, seen most obviously in its complete lack of explicit reference to God. In fact, it is highly improbable that any ancient Jewish reader could have read this story of a remarkable escape of the Jewish people from a threat of total destruction without discerning in it the purpose and power of God to preserve and deliver his chosen people. In any case, the book's canonical context in the biblical history of God's purposes for Israel obliges readers of Scripture to relate it to the outworking of those divine purposes. On the other hand, the book's own failure to supply any explicit theological interpretation of its story, either by the narrator or by the characters in the story, contrasts so strikingly with the rest of the Old Testament narratives that it must be deliberate. We are unlikely to understand Esther correctly unless we take account of it.

However, the overtly secular atmosphere in which the story of Esther seems to unfold need not be held against it. On the contrary, we may find Esther's contemporary relevance for ourselves considerably enhanced by this feature, if we interpret it correctly. It may help us with the very difficult question of discerning the purpose and activity of God in political affairs.

A comparison of the story of Esther with the story of the Exodus will help to make the point.[10] Both are stories of the deliverance of Israel from Gentile power. Esther plays a role at the court of Xerxes which compares in some ways with that of Moses at the court of Pharaoh. But there is also a significant difference between the two stories. In the story of the Exodus the purpose and activity of God are *evident*. Moses as a prophet hears and declares God's purpose. The pillar of cloud and the pillar of fire make God's leading of his people visible. But in the story of Esther there are no such declarations of the divine purpose. Neither Esther nor Mordecai is a prophet to whom God makes his purpose known. There is no one to point authoritatively to the hand of God and no supernatural signs of it. In other words, the writer of Esther depicts the ordinary world of political action, which was the world as he experienced it and the world as we too experience it most of the time, a world without explicit indications of the divine purpose. How do God's people take political action without divine directions, without the pillar of fire or words of prophecy?

The point is not that God is not at work in the story of Esther. The writer takes God's providential care for his people Israel entirely for granted, but he refrains from referring explicitly to it because he wishes the reader to discern it, as the characters *in* such a story are obliged to discern it, without any interpretation provided from outside the story. The question is *how* God is at work and *how* his activity becomes evident. There is one feature of the story which, for the believer, points clearly to the activity of divine providence: the series of remarkable coincidences. The story hinges on a combination of quite unpredictable occurrences, which the human actors in the story could never have deliberately produced, but without which Israel would have perished. Mordecai's discovery of the plot against Xerxes' life (2.22), the vacancy for a queen and Esther's ability to fill it (2.1−18), the king's insomnia on that particular night (6.1), Haman's early arrival at the palace that particular morning (6.4): the combination of these chance events determines the plot. Indeed, it is this piling up of coincidences which makes one feel the story to be historically improbable. But the author has deliberately told a story in which *coincidence* takes the place of miracle as a signal of divine activity. Not that in themselves the coincidences prove anything. But they manifest the hand of God *when* they are seen in the light of the one presupposition about the divine purpose which the author takes for granted and can be sure his readers take for granted: God's commitment to the survival of his people. This was so well known that it can be expressed within the story by Haman's wife Zeresh (6.13), though in a 'non-theological' form, without reference to God, which is both appropriate on her lips and keeps the story free of explicit divine reference. Given that God's purpose is the preservation of his people Israel, the fact that the Jews are preserved, in this story, by coincidental occurrences must point to the activity of divine providence. In this sense, as David Clines puts it, 'God, as a character in the story, becomes more conspicuous the more he is absent'.[11] However, we need to note that this is true only retrospectively. In advance, we know of God's promise to keep his people safe. But how he fulfils it, his providential activity in actual events, emerges only in the course of the story.

In the light of observing this key role of coincidence in the book, we can now notice that human acts contribute to the outcome of the plot in two distinct ways. On the one hand, there are the human actions which make up the coincidental features of the plot. Xerxes, suffering from insomnia, decides to have the court chronicles read to him, and Haman, eager to secure Mordecai's execution as soon as possible, arrives early at the court that morning. These are human actions which *providentially* contribute to the preservation of the Jewish people without the actors having any such intention. Haman, in fact, has quite the opposite intention. But on the other hand, there are human actions which deliberately aim at the preservation of the Jewish people: the actions taken by Mordecai and Esther in chapters 4—5, 7—8. These are just as essential to the redemptive outcome of the plot as the coincidental occurrences are. As David Clines again puts it, 'Without the craft and courage of the Jewish characters the divinely inspired coincidences would have fallen to the ground; and without the coincidences, all the wit in the world would not have saved the Jewish people.'[12] Esther is a story of the *co-operation* between divine providence, manifest in unpredictable events, and the resourceful and courageous actions of Mordecai and Esther.[13]

Now we can understand the full significance of the famous key verse 4.14, in which Mordecai, persuading Esther to take her life in her hands in order to attempt to plead for her people to the king, says: 'If you remain silent at such a time as this, relief and deliverance for the Jews will appear from another quarter, but you and your father's family will perish. Who knows whether it is not for such a time as this that you have come to royal estate?' (NEB). The phrase 'from another quarter' is not, as is sometimes claimed, a covert reference to God.[14] Mordecai does not mean that if Esther does not do something, God will. He means that deliverance for the Jews will occur somehow, whether through Esther's action or by some other means. The one thing of which he is confident is that God will preserve his people, but, in the absence of a message from God, he cannot know *how* he will do so. He cannot know how his or Esther's actions will fit into the divine purpose. It is beginning to look as though Esther's position as queen is providential and that the deliverance of the Jews will come about through the combination of this providential occurrence and Esther's own courageous action on behalf of her people. But he cannot be sure of this, which is clear to us only as the plot unfolds. His 'Who knows whether . . . ?' is not scepticism, but nor has it the confidence of prophecy. It is a hopeful working hypothesis.

This is what Christian political activity is usually like. The politician's own actions rarely *determine* the outcome of events: they are effective only as they interact with a given context and with quite unforeseeable occurrences. The Christian politician must hope to co-operate with divine providence, but at the same time finds himself largely in the dark about the role which his actions will play in the larger divine purpose. In this respect Mordecai's caution is usually more appropriate than a conviction of a God-given destiny to shape history. But this does not mean that the Christian politician's activity is redundant. Esther's courageous activity *turns out* to be a very important element of the way in which God secures the deliverance of his people. Christian politicians must, like Esther, assume the responsibility that they have and act responsibly, trusting the outcome to God. In a world without divine direction, Mordecai and Esther are better models for the Christian politician than Moses and Aaron.

Morality and Power

The book of Esther is about only one political issue: the survival of the Jewish nation in the face of the threat posed by anti-Semitism. It presupposes one element of the divine purpose: God's commitment to the survival of his people Israel. It shows how providential events and responsible political action co-operate to deliver Israel from the threat to her survival. What the book of Esther is *not* about is political ethics. From the fact that the deliverance of Israel was providential we cannot conclude that the steps the human characters take to this end are necessarily morally justified.[15] The hiddenness of God in this book, the fact that the characters have to act without divine *direction*, makes this peculiarly clear. There is no word of God to sanction anything in this book. So here, as in many modern political instances, we must beware of supposing that we cannot welcome an obviously good political result without approving all of the means which produced it. History is not of such a black and white character.

Nevertheless, something must be said about the Jews' slaughter of their enemies which arouses much of the moral indignation over this book. In the first place, there is, of course, no Jewish antagonism to Gentiles as such in the book of Esther. The antagonism between Jews and Gentiles arises out of *Gentile* antagonism to Jews as such, i.e. from anti-Semitism. The book assumes that, anti-Semitism apart, Jews and Gentiles can co-operate in political life, as in Mordecai's action to foil the plot against the king (2.19−23) and his advancement to grand vizier (10.2−3). Those who complain of an antipathy to Gentiles in Esther reveal, as so often in Christian objections to this book, a residual anti-Semitism which instinctively blames Jewish−Gentile conflict on Jewish intolerance of Gentiles rather than Gentile intolerance of Jews. The Holocaust has made such an attitude shocking with reference to modern history, but it seems to survive in judgements about the Old Testament. This is why the Holocaust should help us to understand Esther. It makes is see that the Jews in Esther are a minority ethnic group threatened with genocide. The hostility to them of many of their neighbours can easily be fanned by one malicious politician into a fire which will consume them. To complain of *their* antagonism to Gentiles is to lose all perspective.

Second, the same correction of perspective provided by the Holocaust should warn us against *facile* condemnations of the Jewish 'revenge' in chapter 9. The Jewish defeat of their enemies is portrayed not as revenge, but as self-defence (8.11) and retributive justice (8.13).[16] Those they kill are those who were prepared to carry out the edict of genocide against them (9.2). The retributive justice is crude, but less so than in many other Old Testament examples. In order to disapprove we need to have faced the problems of what forgiveness means in some of the hardest of political cases.

Third, the book of Esther is more realistic about *power* than some of its critics. It recognizes that a threatened minority like the Jews cannot be safe from the hostility of their neighbours without access to political power. Hence the deliverance of the Jews takes place by a reversal of the power situation (9.1),[17] and this is consolidated in Mordecai's exercise of his new-found power in order to protect the Jews (10.3). This last verse of the book (10.3) is an appropriate conclusion because it shows how, for the time being at least, the Jews can remain safe from the type of threat represented by Haman's plan. In an absolute despotism where so much depends on who has the king's favour, this is how things work.

From this point of view, the significance of the establishment of the state of Israel by survivors of the Holocaust can be understood. The alleged right of an ethnic group to political independence in a land of their own and the supposed religious right of the Jews to this particular land may be highly questionable.[18] But the significance of the Jewish recovery of statehood as (in the light of the Holocaust) the political means of Jewish survival is much harder to deny. That the enlightened societies of the modern West could protect Jews against the threats of anti-Semitism was thrown into radical doubt not only by the Holocaust itself, but by the culpable indifference with which the Holocaust was regarded at the time by Nazi Germany's democratic enemies. Just as in Mordecai's time Jewish survival seemed to require Jewish participation in the power-structure of the Persian Empire, so in the modern world of nation states Jewish survival seemed to require the power of self-determination in the form of a Jewish national state. Admittedly, the state of Israel is a highly ambiguous phenomenon, not only because of its consequences for Palestinians, who have experienced it as colonization and displacement, but also because of its religious consequences for Jews themselves. The Jewish emergence from powerlessness has made Israel once again, as in the days of Saul (1 Sam. 8.5), a nation like all the nations, and her religious vocation is compromised by her identity as a secular state.[19] Yet the claims of the argument for survival should not be underestimated. The Zionist tendency to see the world as deeply imbued with a permanent potential for anti-Semitism may easily seem exaggerated to the non-Jew, but it has behind it a history of evil already presaged in the book of Esther and culminating less than half a century ago in one of the most criminal of political crimes.

The *limitation* of the political outlook of the book of Esther is that it does no more than envisage a solution to its problem—the vulnerability of the Jews—within the existing political structure. The power-situation is simply reversed. Anti-Semitism is eliminated by the elimination of the anti-Semites, and Mordecai replaces Haman in power. Thus, despite the implicit, ironic critique of the system of Persian despotism which the narrative embodies, in the end the system is pragmatically accepted and used for the protection of the Jews. This is not untypical of the Old Testament's acceptance and adaptation of existing political systems and structures. Moreover, it was, of course, the most that realistically could be expected for the Jews in the diaspora situation. Mordecai stands in the tradition of Joseph and Daniel: Jews who held office with integrity in pagan empires with dubious political records. But with the advantages of realism goes a limitation of vision. In the teaching of Jesus, on the other hand, we find a radical critique of the kind of power the Gentile empires exercised, requiring not a mere reversal of the power-situation but a reversal of values (Mark 10.42—4). The tension between pragmatic realism and radical vision has been experienced by Christians in politics ever since Constantine.

A Jewish Book for Christian Readers
To read the book of Esther in relation to modern Jewish history and modern anti-Semitism raises *theological* issues which lie outside our scope here. God's providential protection of his people in Esther contrasts with his apparent abandonment of his people to the Holocaust in a way which raises the most perplexing and agonizing theological questions about providence. The theological status of the Jewish people in the light of the New Testament revelation, as well as the Old, has become, through the history of Christian anti-Semitism, a Christian theological problem which cannot be avoided in the Christian attempt to repent of and renounce anti-Semitism. But these broader issues, vitally important though they are, would take us too far from the specifically political implications of the book of Esther. These are, principally, the right of the Jewish people to survive, a right which is rooted in God's concern for Jewish survival, and, in the face of anti-Semitism, the need for *political* measures to protect this right.

Of course, from one point of view, these issues are an instance of the issues of racism and genocide in general. The Jewish people cannot have special political rights which are not those of other peoples—and not even the Old Testament claims that it does. Gipsies have as much right to survival as a distinct people as Jews do. The people of Cambodia under Pol Pot had as much right to protection against genocide as the Jews under the Nazis did. If a national state is admitted to be an implication of the Jewish people's right to survive, then in principle we must be open to the same argument from Armenians, Kurds, or for that matter Palestinians. To some extent the lack of explicit theology in the book of Esther leaves it open to a generalizing application which would be, as it were, the argument of Amos 9.7 in reverse: Israel's right to survival implies also that of other threatened racial groups.

Yet it is also true that anti-Semitism is a specific phenomenon, whose special features are related, as Esther 3.8 already suggests, to the Jewish people's attempt to remain faithful to the laws given them by the God of Israel, and, later, to Gentile Christian *theological* rejection of the legitimacy of Jewish nationhood. These features do not give the Jews political privilege above other threatened groups, but they give the issue of Jewish survival its particularity, just as different specific features give the survival of Amazonian Indians *its* particularity. However legitimate it may also be to generalize the message of Esther, we should not evade its *primary* reference to the particular issue of anti-Semitism. That this is its primary reference is clear, despite its lack of overt theology, from the account of the institution of the feast of Purim (9.23—32).

Unlike the other great festival of national deliverance, the Passover, Purim was never subject to Christian interpretation. It goes unmentioned in the New Testament, just as the book of Esther goes unquoted. The relative neglect of Esther by the Church down the centuries is not unconnected with the stubbornly Jewish character of the book, its relation to a purely Jewish festival and its concern with the Jewish people precisely in its particular ethnic identity. With its lack of any overt concern with the religious vocation of Israel and its exclusive concentration on the issue of the national survival of the Jews, the message of Esther resisted translation into a religious message of universal application. But it should not escape our notice that the Christian neglect and, later, denigration of Esther coincided with the growth of a Christian anti-Semitism which minimized or even denied the Jewish right of national identity. Esther's relevance for Christians ought to derive, in the first place, from the fact that, while becoming less of a Christian book than almost any other book of the Old Testament, Esther has remained a Jewish book, whose annual reading at Purim, throughout the centuries of persecution, needed no interpretation to make it relevant to contemporary experience. In the light of this history, Christians would do well to read Esther precisely as a Jewish book whose presence in the Christian Bible claims Christian attention. They should read Esther as the book which Jewish inmates of the Nazi death-camps were forbidden to read, but wrote out from memory and read in secret on Purim.[20]

9: The Genesis Flood and the Nuclear Holocaust[1]

The most difficult hermeneutical task is probably that of relating the Bible to the really novel features of the modern world which the Bible does not directly address. All too often Christians who try to see the world in a biblical perspective end up forcing the modern world on to the Procrustean bed of the biblical world (i.e. the world within which and to which the Bible was originally written). Genuinely novel features of the modern world are either reduced to some feature of the biblical world, so that their novelty is not really admitted, or else they are not seen as really important features of the modern world, so that their novelty can be admitted but trivialized. That the modern world is significantly shaped by radically novel features, which the authors of Scripture did not envisage, seems hard to admit because the Bible's ability to speak relevantly to the contemporary world would seem to be to that extent reduced.

We need to develop a hermeneutic which bridges the gap between the original contexts of Scripture and our contemporary context not only by way of similarities but also by way of contrasts, so that these very contrasts can be a means by which the Bible illuminates the theological significance of our contemporary world. In this chapter we shall see how this can be done in relation to a modern issue whose staggering novelty has proved very hard for many people to grasp: the threat posed by modern nuclear weapons. Many parts or themes of the Bible could be usefully related to this issue. We select the Flood narrative (Gen. 6—9) because, as in the previous chapter, this will prove an example of a biblical passage which attains surprising new relevance in relation to a modern issue, and also because it will serve to highlight the full scale of the threat with which nuclear weapons confront us.

The Flood
We begin by attempting to understand the significance of the story

of the Flood in its context in Genesis. For our purposes, we may leave aside the difficult question of the historical origin of the story.[2] Whether, as some modern scholars have supposed,[3] the biblical story and the many similar stories around the world preserve a primeval memory of a cataclysmic event which all but destroyed humanity in prehistoric times, or whether the story originated only in one or more local disasters[4] projected on to a universal scale, is not important. It is not important because the message of the story is not so much that God once brought a universal deluge on the earth, but rather that he will never do so again.[5]

The Flood stories of the world, whatever their origins, reflect early humanity's awareness of the fragility of the conditions which make human life on earth possible. Vast forces of nature, capable of catastrophic destruction, threatened human survival. There was nothing about the natural world itself which guaranteed the continuance of human life within it. In the idiom of the Genesis account, the waters of chaos, which God in creation divided and held back (Gen. 1.6−7) in order to create a space in which living creatures could live, were not abolished but only restrained. 'Chaos remains at the edge of creation, so to speak, as a threatening possibility.'[6] Only God's maintenance of the order of creation prevented the incursion of these forces of destruction. The Flood narrative makes this point graphically by recounting the one occasion on which God released the waters of chaos, from above and below the earth (7.11), so that they were reunited and once more submerged the earth, virtually undoing creation, destroying the works of the fifth and sixth days (7.21−3). But the story of the Flood reaches its goal in God's pledge that this will never happen again (8.21−2; 9.8−17). 'While the earth remains' God guarantees the stability of the natural conditions on which the continuance of human and animal life depends (8.22). Never again will there be natural catastrophe on such a scale as to threaten the very survival of the human race (8.21; 9.11).

Thus the initial hermeneutical key to the Flood story is to appreciate how it speaks to early humanity's awareness of the threat to human life from the uncontrollable, chaotic forces of the universe. As such it complements the account of creation. The Creator, who established the conditions of human and animal life in the beginning, could, as the story of the Flood shows, revoke what he has created, but he has in fact pledged himself never again to do so. Early hearers of the story knew that the natural conditions for human survival could not be taken for granted, as though there were any inherent necessity about them, but were contingent on God's will. But they were also able to trust the Creator's promise, symbolized by the rainbow, that he would protect and maintain his creation. His creative will, his commitment to his creation, was dependable.

An existential sense of human survival as threatened by overwhelming catastrophe must have been most alive very early in human history, and must have been already receding in Old Testament times. For much of historical time the survival of humanity has not been a matter for reflection, outside the special case of the apocalyptic tradition, which has its own rather significant links with the Flood story.[7] Political developments made the survival of one's people or nation the overwhelming preoccupation, beyond which the survival of the race as such was neither really in question nor of any independent interest. (Only in recent history has a novel and remarkable tension and alignment between a threat to national survival and a threat to human survival appeared in the form of the nuclear threat.) Moreover, in modern history until recently, fear of the uncontrollable, destructive forces of nature has steadily given way to a sense of human control over the environment and conditions of human life. 'Consequently,' as Claus Westermann comments, 'while creation was always an important part of the teaching of the church, the flood had no significance at all and for all practical purposes disappeared completely from the proclamation.'[8] Of course, the Flood story could have been used to remind people of the contingency of human survival, but in fact it has rarely been so used because it no longer, in the recent historical past, corresponded to any living apprehension about human survival. But Westermann's further observation suggests that this may be changing: 'It is possible that in a future which will be even more aware than the present of dangers and threats to humanity as a whole, the narrative of the flood will be heard anew.'[9]

Before taking up this possibility, we must notice some other features of the Genesis narrative. It is a story not just about universal destruction, but about universal judgement. The Flood had its origin in God's grief at what his human creation had come to, such that he regretted their creation (6.6—7). The sense of these verses is that God's decision to destroy his own creation was a painful one, a decision more in grief than in anger,[10] but a decision made because the earth was no longer as God created it. 'God saw the earth, and behold, it was corrupt' (6.12) stands in deliberate contrast with Genesis 1.31: 'God saw everything that he had made, and behold, it was very good.' His creation is no longer good because human beings have 'corrupted' or 'destroyed' it: hence he will 'destroy them with the earth' (6.13: the same word is rendered 'corrupt' and 'destroy' in 6.11, 12, 13, 17, RSV).

Specifically, it is with 'violence' that human beings have corrupted the earth (6.11, 13).[11] The development of human civilization is described in Genesis 4 in such a way as to highlight this theme of violence. Though the origins of civilization in Cain's city and the inventions of the sons of Lamech (4.17, 20–2) are not condemned, they are framed by a context of escalating violence which gives the achievements of human civilization a deep ambiguity. Cain, the murderer of his brother, began the disruption of all human brotherhood by violence, but to forestall the escalation of violence God protected him from blood-vengeance, pronouncing sevenfold vengeance on any who should slay Cain (4.14–15). Cain's descendant Lamech, however, broke clean through these divine limitations on violence, bragging to his wives of his power to inflict unlimited revenge (4.23–4). Lamech's song not only follows from the technological inventions of his son (4.22), who doubtless forged swords as well as ploughshares, but also sums up the story of civilization in Genesis 4.17–22:

> The Cain and Abel narrative says that when people created by God live side-by-side in brotherhood there is at the same time the possibility of killing. The song of Lamech indicates that the increased progress activated by the human potential increases the possibility of mutual destruction. With the growth of one's capacities there is a growth of self-assertion and amour-propre that demands retribution without limit for even the smallest injury.[12]

The real significance of the Flood as God's judgement on human corruption of the earth through violence emerges, once again, in God's pledge that such a judgement will not happen again. The preservation of Noah and his family made possible a kind of fresh start to creation after the Flood, but this was not a new creation from which the causes of the human sin which had led to the Flood were eliminated. Although in the New Testament the salvation of Noah became a kind of type of Christian salvation (1 Pet. 3.20—1), it could be no more than a type, because the Flood eliminated only sinners, not sin. Hence God after the Flood (8.21) observes that the inclination of the human heart is evil, just as he had done before the Flood (6.5), but whereas before the Flood this was the ground for destroying humanity, after the Flood it is a situation which God tolerates. *In spite of* human evil, God resolves never again to destroy humanity (8.21). Thus,

> just because the world now stands under the divine mercy, the Flood is unrepeatable. It is not that the reason for the Flood no longer exists, as if the wickedness of the generation of the Flood was greater than that of any subsequent generation. Mankind after the Flood is not different . . . In spite of human sin and violence, God has committed himself to his world.[13]

In this perspective, the strictly unilateral character of the so-called 'Noahic covenant' (9.8—17) is important. No human conditions attach to it. God's pledge to hold back the waters of chaos from now on is unconditional grace.

Thus the Flood narrative reveals that the survival of the human race is not only contingent on the divine will as such, but dependent on the divine mercy and patience.[14] What has been in principle forfeited again and again by sin, is continually given by God's grace in faithfulness to his pledge to Noah. It is against this background of universal mercy that the biblical story of God's purpose for universal redemption unfolds.

So far we have considered the Flood as a story about human survival, but it is also, very prominently, a story about animal survival. The two are bound up together, in that 'humans and the animals stand together in face of catastrophes that threaten life'.[15] Contrary to the way it has sometimes been interpreted, Genesis does not represent the animals as created for the sake of humanity, but it does place them under the responsible and benevolent authority of humanity, to whom, as the dominant species on earth, God has delegated a measure of his own authority on earth (Gen. 1.26, 28).[16] Of all biblical characters it is Noah, in his 'conservationist' role, who best exemplifies the true meaning of this human 'dominion', as exercised in imitation of God's care for his creation. Although Genesis 9.2—5 does give human survival a certain priority over animal survival, even here it is clear that animal life has its own value in the sight of God, which may not be disregarded even in such killing of animals as God permits (9.4). But even more strikingly, the terms of the Noahic covenant constitute a rebuke to the human tendency to see the world in more anthropocentric terms than God does. All the animals are explicitly its beneficiaries alongside Noah and his descendants (9.10, 12, 15, 16). God is concerned for and pledges himself to the survival of the animal creation as well as humanity.[17]

Finally, we should notice that the renewal of the creation mandate to humanity in Genesis 9.1−7 not only indicates a kind of fresh start to creation after the Flood, re-establishing God's creative will for humanity on earth and in relation to the animals, but also expresses this creative will in terms conditioned by the violence which is now a feature of human life. Since God now pledges himself to the survival of human and animal life in spite of this violence, the creation mandate is reformulated to take account of it. Violence must be contained so that it does not endanger human survival. A limited degree of violence now enters the notion of human dominion over the animals (9.2−5), but only in the interests of human survival. Similarly, the violence of man against man is to be restrained by God's permission for limited retaliation (9.6), so that murder shall not lead to the unlimited violence of the blood-feud, which always in ancient society threatened to go on for ever. Thus God now permits such limited violence as will enable humanity to multiply and populate the earth (9.1, 7) in the face of both animal and internecine violence. With biblical hindsight, of course, we can recognize in this a kind of holding operation, with a view to God's redemptive strategy for the transformation of human hearts. Unlike the conditional grace of the Noahic covenant, however, it is a holding operation which God entrusts to humanity to carry out. There is no guarantee that it will work for ever.

The Nuclear Holocaust
In very recent times the sense that the actual survival of the human race on earth is threatened has begun to become once again part of general awareness of the human condition. But it has emerged in a form significantly different from the ancient form to which the story of the Flood originally spoke. Whereas in ancient times it reflected humanity's vulnerability to the uncontrollable, destructive forces of nature, in modern times it reflects humanity's unprecedented control over the forces of nature.

Scientific and technological progress have placed modern

humanity in a very different relationship to the natural world and the animal creation from that which is presupposed in Genesis 9. We no longer live largely within the given conditions of the natural world, but control and direct the forces of nature, and are continually adapting the natural world to make it a more favourable environment for human life. Even though we are still vulnerable to natural catastrophes, increasingly we are even able to reduce the disastrous effects of these, while such shattering phenomena as famine in Africa are in fact predictable and preventable, so that they no longer reflect human helplessness before the forces of nature but rather human selfishness, negligence and greed. However, the deep ambiguity of human civilization, as already perceived in its origins in Genesis 4, has become more and more apparent in the results of modern technological advance. The same process which has relieved so much human suffering has also made possible the sickening cruelties of twentieth-century wars and tyrannies. The ecological crisis has revealed how the same mastery over nature which has adapted nature for our benefit and freed us, to some extent, from dependence on uncontrollable factors in the natural world, has come at the same time to threaten the natural conditions on which our survival depends. By taking into our own hands the management of the conditions of human life on earth, we have taken on the responsibility for maintaining or destroying them.

The terrifying ambiguity of modern humanity's mastery of nature becomes nowhere so obvious as in the nuclear bomb. *We* can now do what the Flood did. What in Noah's day only the forces of nature under the sole control of God could do, human beings can now do. We can let loose the forces of chaos and undo God's creation. Whereas before the Flood human violence 'destroyed' the earth in the sense of 'corrupting' it (6.11—12), human violence now threatens to destroy the earth in the sense in which God destroyed it in the Flood (6.13, 17). The threat to the survival of the human race now comes directly from ourselves. As Jonathan Schell says, by inventing the capacity for self-extinction as a species, human beings 'have caused a basic change in the circumstances in which life was given us, which is to say that we have altered the human condition'.[18]

No one, of course, can be entirely sure what the effects of the use of nuclear weapons on a significant scale would be. In particular, it is not clear how far the southern hemisphere might escape the devastating effects of a nuclear war in the northern hemisphere. But when full account is taken not simply of the immediate devastation caused by the nuclear explosions and radiation, but also of the large-scale atmospheric effects of the 'nuclear winter' and long-term environmental effects, including irreparable damage to the ozone layer, it is clear that any sizeable exchange of nuclear weapons could constitute a real threat to human survival. Not every possible nuclear war would terminate human history, but that it is now within human capacity to render the planet no longer habitable for human beings, or indeed for most other forms of life, cannot be doubted.[19]

The radical novelty of this threat of human *self*-destruction is such that the Bible does not envisage it. (The Bible's apocalyptic scenario of world destruction is no more a case of human *self*-destruction than is the Flood.) So at this point we must avoid the Evangelical hermeneutical temptation of emphasizing similarities at the expense of the differences between situations addressed in the Bible and contemporary situations. This is cheap relevance. It seeks to make the Bible seem relevant to modern people, but does so by distorting its actual message. The Bible's real relevance to contemporary people can be perceived only by fully recognizing the extent to which we find ourselves in circumstances different from those it directly addresses. Just as a moment's thought will make it clear why Hagar cannot be a biblical precedent for so-called surrogate motherhood, as currently practised, so it should already be clear that the nuclear holocaust would not be another Flood. But on the other hand, careful attention to the contrasting parallelism between the Flood and the nuclear holocaust can help us to put the nuclear threat in a biblical perspective.

In the first place, we should be clear that the Noahic covenant does not cover the threat of nuclear holocaust in the sense of providing a divine guarantee that the holocaust will not happen. God's pledge not to destroy the earth is not a promise to prevent human beings from doing so; the possibility that they could had not entered the horizon of Genesis 9.[20] On the other hand, the Noahic covenant *is* relevant to the nuclear situation, in that it assures us of God's commitment to human survival on earth. This has important implications. It means, for example, that a nuclear policy which risks human extinction is not some kind of heroic choice of death in preference to surrender of freedom or principle, but a direct rejection of the value which God himself puts on his human creation. To risk human extinction in a policy of nuclear retaliation can certainly not appeal to the divine permission for retaliation (9.6) which was designed for the quite contrary purpose of protecting human survival against the threat of escalating violence. Moreover, any attempted justification of nuclear retaliation which points to the supposed wickedness of the enemy, is not only an ideological abuse of moral categories: it also knows nothing of the gracious God of the Noahic covenant, who tolerates sin and withholds judgement because he is committed to the survival of his human creation in spite of its wickedness.

God's own commitment to human survival should form a kind of background to our Christian thinking about the nuclear issue and our Christian peacemaking activity. It does not mean that, in a situation in which human survival is, in a very important sense, in human hands, we can *presume* on God's providence to prevent the holocaust. In this situation, God's tolerance may, simply by leaving us to the consequences of our sin, become his judgement. In other words, God's commitment to human survival cannot relieve human beings of their own responsibility to ensure it. But it does assure those who work for peace that their efforts are in the direction of the divine purpose in history. Their responsible activity can be rooted in prayer to and trust in the God who is on their side because he is on the side of humanity as such.[21]

It is in the light of the theological meaning of the Flood narrative that the full horror of nuclear weapons becomes apparent. They threaten to destroy God's creation which God himself, in spite of his grief at the extent to which it is already spoilt by human sin, has pledged himself to preserve. They threaten not only the human creation, created in God's image, but also the animal creation for which God has made humanity responsible and which he made Noah responsible for preserving even through the Flood. At a time when human dominance on earth already means the extinction of animal species at the rate of three a day, we have come a long way from the situation of primitive humanity when wild animals were a major threat to human survival (9.2). It is a measure of our unbiblical anthropocentrism that the nuclear issue is regularly discussed as though only human beings would be affected.[22] We have forgotten that human dignity, our creation in God's image, consists not in our liberty to disregard the rest of creation, but precisely in our exercise of responsible care for the rest of creation. Weapons which can reduce God's world to a smoking, poisonous waste, habitable only by insects, must be assessed in a theological context much broader than the ethics of the just war. 'More than human blood cries out to God.'[23]

The nuclear threat expresses human rebellion against the creation mandate, both in its original form in Genesis 1.28 and in its reformulated form in Genesis 9.1−7. It threatens to destroy the creation for which God has made humanity responsible. It threatens to break all bounds of violence with a boast, like Lamech's, of unlimited retaliation, thereby both transgressing the limits and defeating the purpose of the strictly limited violence permitted by Genesis 9.2−6. In seizing the godlike power to destroy God's creation, which God himself in the Noahic covenant pledged himself not to use, nuclear weapons express humanity's refusal to fulfil the divine image in imitation of God and their determination instead to be gods in their own right. It is symbolically appropriate that in the nuclear winter no rainbows will be visible, since human beings will have taken it upon themselves to override God's creative will for the survival of his human and non-human creation.

Finally, I suggest that the Flood story can help us towards a kind of new quality of awareness of God and the world and ourselves, which the novelty and the gravity of the nuclear situation demand. To read the Flood narrative with sensitivity to its original import is to acquire a renewed sense of the world in which we live as God's gift to us. As we see its destruction withheld only by God's patience and mercy, we find the world we take for granted becomes once again the world continually granted to us by God's grace. With Noah we lose the world and find it again, finding it the more valuable in its newly experienced relationship to God. Serious confrontation with the nuclear threat can be the occasion for a similar experience of losing and finding. Contemplating what would be lost, we experience with fresh reality the goodness and beauty of the world which God has not yet allowed us to destroy, just as a person reprieved from terminal illness experiences the gratuitous joy of living with new intensity. And finding the world, so to speak, given back to us for the time being, we learn to share God's own commitment to its preservation. The relatively novel element in experiencing the world in the face of the nuclear threat is that we find the world again both as God's gift *and* as our responsibility. In this way the experience becomes not some kind of religious escape from the urgent responsibilities of the nuclear age, but the source of a Christian perspective in which we can properly exercise those responsibilities.

10: The Political Christ

A Concluding Reflection

Jesus Christ is the centre of the canon of Scripture. All the themes of Scripture converge on him and find their final and fullest significance with reference to him. All Christian study of Scripture must constantly return to him if it is to read Scripture correctly. So can we read, not just certain passages of the Gospels, but Jesus himself politically? To interpret Jesus and his significance in *purely* political terms would be to reduce Jesus. But we should also be reducing Jesus if we were to exclude the political dimension of his life and fate. Because the Kingdom of God he served embraces the whole of human life, and because he identified in love with human beings whose lives were affected by political structures and policies, his mission impinged on the political along with other dimensions of life. Politics, as we have observed a number of times, is not everything; nor is the political dimension a watertight, autonomous sphere of life; it interacts with all other dimensions of life. Thus we may expect to find that Jesus' life, death and resurrection, while not reducible to politics, have a political dimension.

The Praxis of Jesus
Jesus in his ministry proclaimed the coming Kingdom of God and *practised its presence*. That is, he anticipated the future hope of the unrestricted, uncontested sovereignty of God, by extending God's rule in the present and inviting people to live within it. This was not the Kingdom of God in its fullest, eschatological sense, but it was a preliminary presence of the Kingdom within history. Preliminary, because it made itself felt in relation to evil and suffering and death, triumphing over them but not yet eliminating them from the world. But a real presence of the Kingdom, because in Jesus' praxis the *characteristics* of God's rule could be identified. In summary, the rule of God as Jesus' praxis embodied it was the sovereignty of God's gracious and fatherly love. In more detail, it was:

in relation to demonic oppression, conquest;
in relation to misrepresentation of God's rule, sharp rebuke;
in relation to selfish complacency, warning;
in relation to sin and failure, forgiveness and assurance of love;
in relation to sickness, healing;
in relation to material need, provision of daily bread;
in relation to exclusion, welcoming inclusion;
in relation to desire for power, an example of humble and loving
service;
in relation to death, life;
in relation to false peace, painful division, but in relation to
enmity, reconciliation.

These general characteristics—not an exhaustive list—are gathered from the stories and the sayings in the Gospels, which are themselves the irreplaceable indications of the nature of God's Kingdom.

The key to the way that Jesus actualized God's rule is his loving identification with people.[1] As the Son of God his Father, who himself lived out of his experience of his Father's love, Jesus was able to bring God's love powerfully to bear on people's lives. But this could not happen in a purely generalizing way, by preaching an indiscriminate message of God's benevolence towards everyone. God's love through Jesus reached people in their actual, very different life-situations, because Jesus in love identified with people, understood and felt their problems and needs. Only so could God's love reach into and change their lives. While he practised God's universal love for all people, Jesus could do so only by constantly particularizing it as God's love for this or that person in his or her particular situation.

This means that, on the one hand, Jesus' loving identification with people knew no limits, but, on the other hand, he did not identify with everyone in the same way. It is important to keep these two sides of the coin in mind. In the first place, Jesus' love excluded no one. He held aloof neither from the outcasts of society nor from the respectable people who were scandalized by the company he kept. He dined with tax-collectors and sinners, but also with Pharisees. The recipients of his healing included the blind beggar Bartimaeus, a Samaritan leper, the servant of a Roman centurion, and a slave of the high priest sent to arrest him. He raised from the dead not only the son of the widow of Nain, who without male relatives lacked all economic support, but also the daughter of the no doubt well-to-do Jairus, whose grief was not to be despised because of his social importance. Jesus' disciples and loyal friends included the partners in a small fishing business, a tax-collector, a former demoniac, the wife of Herod's estate manager, and a wealthy aristocrat. Even Jesus' highly critical confrontations with religious leaders do not fall outside his loving solidarity with all people: they were the only way he could bring home to such people the character and demands of God's love as it impinged on their particular situation. Thus Jesus' loving identification crossed all barriers and reached people in all the varieties of the human condition, people divided by all the differences—physical, social, economic, political—which divide people into sexes, classes, races, ages, states of health and so on.

However, it is equally important to notice, secondly, that Jesus did not identify with all these people in the same way. He met their actual, very different needs for God's solidarity with them as they themselves were. He touched and healed lepers. He found the rich young ruler a good and upright person, and for that reason asked him to give his wealth to the poor. He refused to condemn the woman taken in adultery, but was unrestrained in his attacks on the Pharisees. In considering how Jesus particularized God's love in different ways for different people, there are three aspects of special relevance to our political concern.

In the first place, Jesus made no artificial distinctions between the dimensions of human life and had no rigid policy of reaching people in one or other dimension of life, but appreciated people's life-situation as a whole and acted appropriately. The healing of lepers well illustrates the point. By healing the disease Jesus changed the life of a leper in many dimensions. Since leprosy entailed isolation from the rest of society, both because of the contagious nature of the disease and also because of the ritual uncleanness involved, restoration to physical health brought with it restoration to the social and religious community. By risking ritual defilement and *touching* a leper, Jesus expressed his healing not only of disease but also of human community. Moreover, at least in the case of those, like the Samaritan leper, who responded with recognition and gratitude to God, what Jesus mediated through the healing action, with its physical, social and economic effects, was a fresh experience of God's love, which encompassed all dimensions of life. But if the point of entry, so to speak, for

God's love in the case of lepers was physical healing, for the Samaritan woman, to take a different example, it was elsewhere: initially in Jesus' crossing the barriers of social superiority which separated men from women and Jews from Samaritans, subsequently in his bringing to the surface the woman's failure in married life.

Second, although Jesus certainly met people as individuals, he also appreciated the extent to which they belonged to specific social groups. Some of the people Jesus met emerge as individuals in the gospel stories, some remain for us representatives of social groups, which the Gospels also mention in general terms as groups with which Jesus associated: tax-collectors, disabled beggars, lepers, Sadducees, prostitutes, the rich, the poor, and so on. What life was like for a member of any of these groups was very considerably determined by his or her membership of that group, and so Jesus' loving identification with people had to include his awareness of their place in the social and economic structures of first-century Palestine. God's love would not be fully particularized if it reached a tax-collector simply as a tax-collector, and not as *this* tax-collector, Zacchaeus or Levi; but, on the other hand, it could not reach Zacchaeus or Levi without taking full account of his being a tax-collector. Thus politics, which deals with structures and social groups more than with individuals as individuals, has a place in our discipleship of Jesus. It cannot fully implement Jesus' particular concern for each individual he met, but it can be a vehicle for his concern for people as members of social groups whose lives are shaped by the structures of society.

Third, it is in this context of Jesus' loving identification with all in different ways that we must consider the claim that Jesus' praxis displayed a *preferential* concern for the poor. It would be better to speak of Jesus' special concern for the marginalized, those who were excluded from society to a greater or lesser degree, since by no means all these people were economically poor. Tax-collectors most certainly were not, and indeed their despised position in society was partly because they had grown rich, by dubious means, at others' expense. Yet they were prominent among those with whom Jesus was notorious for associating. The key to Jesus' 'preference' for various groups must be their relative exclusion, for social, economic and religious reasons, from the society of God's people. Thus, he treated women, who were very much second-class citizens in Jewish society of the time, with exceptional respect, implicitly acknowledging their full and equal status in Israel. People whose permanent physical handicaps reduced them to beggary and pushed them to the social and economic margins of society were prominent among the people he healed. But he also made friends with the moral outcasts—tax-collectors and prostitutes—making a special point, by accepting hospitality and sharing meals, of including them in the social bonds of the renewed Israel as he envisaged it. In his deliberate attempt to reach those who were shunned and forgotten by everyone else, he sought out the most hopeless cases of all: the lepers, whom society treated as more or less already corpses, and the demoniacs, whose condition seemed virtually to exclude them from humanity altogether.

Jesus' special concern for the marginalized people was not a neglect of others. Rather, Jesus' mission was to reach all with God's loving solidarity and thereby create loving solidarity among all. But for this purpose his special concern had to be the inclusion of those who were excluded from human solidarity and those who felt excluded from God's solidarity. Those who excluded others from the solidarity of God's people could properly learn God's solidarity with themselves only along with his solidarity with the people they excluded. Not only for the sake of the tax-collectors and sinners, then, but actually also for the sake of the Pharisees, Jesus identified himself with tax-collectors and sinners.

Jesus' vision of the Kingdom of God, provisionally present in a fragmentary way through his ministry, was of a society without the privilege and status which favour some and exclude others. Thus those who had no status in society as it was then constituted were given a conspicuous place in society as God's rule was reconstituting it through Jesus. This ensured that the rich and the privileged could find their place only alongside the poor and the underprivileged. The last became first and the first became last so that there should be no status or privilege at all. Similarly, in a society where righteousness was treated by some as a status which privileged them and excluded others, Jesus made it clear that notorious sinners, who could make no claim to righteous status, had a rightful place in the Kingdom of God's forgiving grace. Those who considered themselves righteous could then take their place only by abandoning the privilege of righteousness in the solidarity of grace. Finally, Jesus, who loved children, made a small child his model of citizenship in God's Kingdom, because children had no social status. To enter the Kingdom, all must become like the little child. Like his preference for children, Jesus' preference for the tax-collectors and the beggars was not against the others, but for them. The others must abandon status in order with Jesus to enter the solidarity of the unrighteous, the poor and the children. There was no other route to the Kingdom of God in which no one is less than or thinks himself more than a neighbour to all others.

The Cross of Jesus

Crucifixion was a common fate in the ancient world. Yet it is a remarkable fact that the gospel narratives of *Jesus'* crucifixion are the longest, most detailed *accounts* of a crucifixion which can be found in ancient literature.[2] Ancient writers usually refer to crucifixion only in passing, rarely dwelling on the details, and many authors who should have had occasion to refer to it avoid mentioning it at all.

It is worth pondering the reasons for this neglect. In the first place, crucifixion was regarded as the most horrible way to die: a form of execution deliberately made as painful as possible, an excruciatingly slow death, exposed to public shame and mockery. The cultured, literary world wanted nothing to do with it. Not that they wanted it abolished: they took it for granted that this most cruel of judicial sanctions was essential as a deterrent to maintain civilized society. But they put it out of mind, lest it spoil the image of Roman civilization as humane and beneficent. They engaged in a kind of double-think characteristic of many societies: on the one hand, propagating and really believing in an idealized picture of their society as the home of civilized values, while, on the other hand, knowing that this civilization is kept in being by a system of torture and terror. Crucifixion was and had to be offensively public. So much the more resolutely was it banished from the literature and culture in which the Roman Empire celebrated its glory. Great generals like Julius Caesar, great provincial governors like Pliny, who regularly ordered crucifixions, wrote up their memoirs with never a mention of the fact. It was not what they wished to remember or be remembered for.

However, a second reason why ancient literature rarely dwelt on crucifixion reinforces the first: the people who were crucified were not people who mattered. Crucifixion was for the lower classes, foreigners, slaves. It was the penalty for political crimes against the state, for violent robbery, and for rebellious slaves. It maintained the authority of the state and the structure of a slave-owning society. It secured peace and prosperity for the majority by barbarous treatment of others. Crucifixion could be forgotten precisely because it was a way of forgetting people, a way of excluding from society those who would disturb its conscience or its security, a way of denying humanity to the 'others', a way of reducing their humanity to carrion.

The illusion of a civilized society had to be maintained by forgetting its victims. Crucifixion was the way of removing them, rendering them nothing; and so that they might be well and truly forgotten, crucifixion itself was not discussed. Hence the peculiar offensiveness of the Christian message of Jesus the crucified God: a God who suffered execution like a rebel or a slave, a God who was one of the victims who do not matter and ought to be forgotten. Such a God was not only ridiculous, but brutally offensive: he assaulted the illusions of Roman society head-on.

In his crucifixion Jesus identified himself unequivocally and finally with the victims. He suffered their fate of being made nothing in order to restore their humanity as people who are something. He joined the forgotten, but he himself and the story of his crucifixion were remembered. Roman society and the Roman state tried hard to suppress the memory of this crucified man as they suppressed the memory of others, but in his case they failed. His crucifixion has become the best-known fact of Roman history. He is remembered, and his solidarity with all the forgotten victims brings them to remembrance too.

Jesus could have avoided suffering, but in obedience to his mission of communicating God's love he chose the path which inevitably made him one of the victims. As such he suffered in the same way as many others. Stripped of all human dignity, exhausted by continuous pain, helpless before his executioners and the jeering onlookers, deserted by friends and by his God, Jesus was reduced to sheer victim. Yet his suffering did not, as suffering often does, turn him in on himself and deprive him of the spiritual strength to be concerned for others. On the contrary, his loving concern reached all the people around him as he hung dying: his fellow victims on the crosses beside him, his mother in her grief, even his executioners, for whom he prayed forgiveness. Because he suffered out of love and loved in his suffering, the crucified Jesus was God's loving solidarity with all who suffer victimization.

Of course, it is of central importance to the Christian gospel that the crucified Jesus died in loving solidarity with all of us, the executioner and the bystander as well as the victim. On the cross he meets us all in the final truth of the human condition as such: our condemnation, failure, suffering and mortality. But it is also important that he died a victim of a political system. We must not give his death a meaning which is indifferent to the processes and structures by which some human beings make victims of others. We must not forget that his loving solidarity with all made him a victim with some at the hands of others. It is as one of the victims that in his love he reaches all of us.

For those of us who are not ourselves victims, that means that Jesus cannot be rightly remembered today without bringing to remembrance also his fellow victims in the world today. He requires us to see the world from their perspective, renouncing the comfortable perspectives of societies which have so many ways of leaving people to suffer, excluding and forgetting them. His solidarity with the victim forbids us to ignore the sufferings of the forgotten victims, and forbids us also to distort their sufferings by means of self-justifying illusions. The pretence, for example, that the imposition of suffering on some people is worthwhile for the sake of the greater good of the rest of us cannot survive the disillusioning effect of Jesus' cross. By insisting that we remember the victims and adopt their perspective, it exposes for what they are all the terrible ideologies—of right, left and centre—which justify suffering: 'of course' progress has its victims, 'of course' the weak will go to the wall, 'of course' the defence of our society will cause innocent suffering, 'of course' the price of the revolution will be innocent suffering. Any ideology which encourages us to ignore or to minimize the sufferings of some in the interests of others is forbidden us by the cross. The crucified God is always with the victims, even with the victims of the victims.

The Resurrection of Jesus

During his ministry Jesus took up, in proclamation and practice, many of the prophetic hopes of the Old Testament. In a preliminary way the expectations of a time when God's rule would prevail against all evil and suffering were being actualized. But the culmination of the prophetic hopes was the hope for the resurrection of the dead, the hope that God would triumph even over 'the last enemy' death in a new creation no longer subject to mortality. This was the furthest conceivable extent of God's rule, and so the hope of resurrection included and represented all the Old Testament promises for the future. The significance of Jesus' resurrection, therefore, was as a kind of breakthrough to the eschatological Kingdom, to that final condition of the world which is God's perfect will for his creation. The fragmentary anticipations of the Kingdom in Jesus' ministry were surpassed by this entry into glory, beyond all evil, suffering and death. But, of course, it was Jesus only who entered the glory of the new creation, one man as pioneer for the rest. His resurrection was God's definitive promise of the resurrection of others and of the Kingdom of glory into which all creation will be assumed.

The risen Jesus is our future. He beckons us forward to the goal of creation and gives all Christian activity the character of hopeful movement into the future which God has promised. Not that we ourselves can achieve that future. Resurrection makes that clear: we who ourselves end in death cannot achieve the new creation out of death. The Kingdom in its final glory lies beyond the reach of our history, in the hands of the God who interrupted our history by raising Jesus from death. This transcendence of the Kingdom beyond our achievement must be remembered. But in Jesus God has given us the Kingdom not only as hope for the final future but also to anticipate in the present. As the vision of God's perfect will for his creation it is the inspiration of all Christian efforts to change the world for the better. In relation to our political activity, it is a double-edged sword, cutting through both our pretensions and our excuses. On the one hand, as the goal we do not reach, it passes judgement on all our political projects and achievements, forbids us the dangerous utopian illusion of having paradise within our grasp, keeps us human, realistic, humble and dissatisfied. On the other hand, as the goal we must anticipate, it lures us on beyond all our political achievements, forbids us disillusioned resignation to the status quo, keeps us dissatisfied, hopeful, imaginative, and open to new possibilities.

However, Christian hope, founded on the resurrection of Jesus, is also hope that has been interrupted by the cross of Jesus and re-established only as hope for the victims with whom the crucified Jesus was identified. The progress which creates victims and the progress which leaves the victims behind have nothing to do with the Kingdom of God as Jesus defines it. Only in solidarity with the victims can his future be our future.

Notes

Introduction

1 Quoted in R. McAfee Brown, *Unexpected News: Reading the Bible with Third World Eyes* (Philadelphia: Westminster Press, 1984), p. 163.

Chapter 1

1 See C. Westermann, *Genesis 1–11: A Commentary* (London: SPCK, 1984), pp. 514–18.
2 C. J. H. Wright, *Living as the People of God: The Relevance of Old Testament Ethics* (Leicester: Inter-Varsity Press, 1983), pp. 40–5.
3 A. Dumas, *Political Theology and the Life of the Church* (London: SCM Press, 1978), pp. 68–9.
4 There is a useful discussion in W. M. Swartley, *Slavery, Sabbath, War, and Women* (Scottdale, Pennsylvania: Herald Press, 1983), chapter 1.

Chapter 2

1 J. Morgenstern, 'The Decalogue of the Holiness Code', *Hebrew Union College Annual* 26 (1955), p. 12.
2 This list is from D. Patrick, *Old Testament Law* (Atlanta: John Knox Press, 1985), p. 162. Morgenstern, 'Decalogue', attempts, with only limited success, to show that the original core of the chapter was a decalogue related to, but not identical with, *the* Decalogue.
3 For this paragraph, see Patrick, *Old Testament Law*, pp. 198–200.
4 C. J. H. Wright, *Living as the People of God: The Relevance of Old Testament Ethics* (Leicester: Inter-Varsity Press, 1983), pp. 51–9.
5 J. V. Taylor, *Enough is Enough* (London: SCM Press, 1975), p. 51.
6 See G. J. Wenham, 'Leviticus 27.2–8 and the Price of Slaves', *Zeitschrift für die alttestamentliche Wissenschaft* 90 (1978), pp. 264–5.
7 I borrow the phrase from *Changing Britain: Social Diversity and Moral Unity: A Study for the Board for Social Responsibility* (London: Church House, 1987), chapter 4, which is a useful discussion of the task.
8 The translation, 'damages must be paid', is uncertain, but makes good sense in the context. It was suggested by E. A. Speiser, *Oriental and Biblical Studies* (Philadelphia: University of Pennsylvania Press, 1967), pp. 128–31, and adopted by M. Noth, *Leviticus* (Old Testament Library; London: SCM Press, 1977), p. 143, and G. J.

Notes

Wenham, *The Book of Leviticus* (New International Commentary on the Old Testament; London: Hodder & Stoughton, 1979), p. 270, though rejected by J. Milgrom, 'The Betrothed Slave-girl, Lev. 19.20–2', *Zeitschrift für die alttestamentliche Wissenschaft* 89 (1977), p. 43, n. 2.

9   This translation is from Wenham, *Leviticus*, p. 262.

10 It should be emphasized that the passage is very obscure, and what follows is no more than one possible reconstruction of its meaning.

11 The death penalty for adultery may not often have been carried out: cf. H. McKeating, 'Sanctions against Adultery in Ancient Israelite Society, with some Reflections on Methodology in the Study of Old Testament Ethics', *Journal for the Study of the Old Testament* 11 (1979), pp. 57–72. An alternative redress for the husband of an adulterous wife was divorce: Deuteronomy 24.1; Jeremiah 3.8; Hosea 2.2–3. Since the Old Testament law is not as such a statute-book for use in the courts, we cannot assume that all laws were necessarily intended to be enforced: see Patrick, *Old Testament Law*, p. 199; J. Goldingay, *Theological Diversity and the Authority of the Old Testament* (Grand Rapids: Eerdmans, 1987), p. 164.

12 See Wenham, *Leviticus*, pp. 108–9.

13 The point is argued fully by Milgrom, 'The Betrothed Slave-girl'.

14 Milgrom, 'The Betrothed Slave-girl', p. 49.

15 See Wright, *Living*, pp. 178–82; H. W. Wolff, *Anthropology of the Old Testament* (London: SCM Press, 1974), pp. 199–205.

16 Nor did free women have equal status with free men.

17 Goldingay, *Theological Diversity*, p. 154; cf. pp. 153–66 for the topic of this whole paragraph.

18 cf. F. C. Fensham, 'Widow, Orphan, and the Poor in Ancient Near Eastern Legal and Wisdom Literature', in J. L. Crenshaw, ed., *Studies in Ancient Israelite Wisdom* (New York: Ktav, 1976), pp. 161–71; H. K. Havice, *The Concern for the Widow and the Fatherless in the Ancient Near East: A Case Study in Old Testament Ethics* (unpublished Ph.D. dissertation, Yale University, 1978).

19 cf. R. A. Guelich, *The Sermon on the Mount: A Foundation for Understanding* (Waco, Texas: Word Books, 1982), p. 250.

20 Wenham, *Leviticus*, pp. 266–7.

21 It is worth noting that (as L. T. Johnson, 'The Use of Leviticus 19 in the Letter of James', *Journal of Biblical Literature* 101 (1982), pp. 391–401, demonstrates) James, who calls Leviticus 19.18b 'the royal law' (Jas. 2.8), i.e. the law of God's Kingdom, treats the whole passage Leviticus 19.12–18 as an explication of this law, though it needs the interpretation given it by Jesus (as in Jas. 5.12).

22 Wenham, *Leviticus*, p. 263.

23 cf. Guelich, *Sermon on the Mount*, pp. 225–7, 253; V. P. Furnish, *The Love Command in the New Testament* (Nashville/New York: Abingdon, 1972), pp. 46–7.

Notes

Chapter 3

1 For the reasons for this identification, see C. G. Rasmussen in *The International Standard Bible Encyclopedia*, ed. G. W. Bromiley, vol. 3 (Grand Rapids: Eerdmans, 1986), p. 277.

2 But cf. the role of the mother in Proverbs 1.8; 6.20.

3 See below, note 4.

4 J. B. Pritchard, ed., *Ancient Near Eastern Texts Relating to the Old Testament* (Princeton: Princeton University Press, 1955), pp. 414–18; W. K. Simpson, ed., *The Literature of Ancient Egypt* (New Haven/London: Yale University Press, 1973), pp. 180–92; and for a discussion of the work, see W. McKane, *Proverbs: A New Approach* (Old Testament Library; London: SCM Press, 1970), pp. 67–75. See also the Instruction of Amenemhet, in Pritchard, *Ancient Near Eastern Texts*, pp. 418–19; Simpson, *Literature*, pp. 193–7.

5 Some scholars have questioned the authenticity of the work, but this is not relevant to our interest in it here.

6 Simpson, *Literature*, p. 183.

7 On the hierarchical presuppositions of concern for the underprivileged in Egyptian literature, see H. K. Havice, *The Concern for the Widow and the Fatherless in the Ancient Near East: A Case Study in Old Testament Ethics* (unpublished Ph.D. dissertation, Yale University, 1978), chapter 1.

8 cf. Proverbs 8.15–16; 16.12; 20.8, 26; 25.4–5.

9 cf. David's judgement on the putative case put to him by Nathan: 2 Samuel 12.1–6.

10 McKane, *Proverbs*, pp. 411–12.

11 Job also claims to have been a father to orphans (Job 31.18), though the context is not judicial.

12 On this subject (with varying assessments of it), see W. Eichrodt, *Theology of the Old Testament*, vol. 1 (London: SCM Press, 1961), pp. 436–56; H. W. Wolff, *Anthropology of the Old Testament* (London: SCM Press, 1974), pp. 192–8; G. E. Mendenhall, 'The Monarchy', *Interpretation* 29 (1975), pp. 155–70; P. D. Miller, 'The Prophetic Critique of Kings', *Ex Auditu* 2 (1986), pp. 82–95.

13 See the already classic sociological study of N. K. Gottwald, *The Tribes of Yahweh: A Sociology of the Religion of Liberated Israel 1250–1050* (London: SCM Press, 1980), with discussion in 'Theological Issues in *The Tribes of Yahweh* by N. K. Gottwald: Four Critical Reviews', in N. K. Gottwald, ed., *The Bible and Liberation: Political and Social Hermeneutics* (Maryknoll, New York: Orbis Books, 1983), pp. 166–89; C. J. H. Wright, 'The Use of the Bible in Social Ethics III: The Ethical Relevance of Israel as a Society', *Transformation* 1/4 (1984), pp. 11–21.

14 Babylonian Talmud, *Sanhedrin* 43a.

Notes

Chapter 4

1 In all probability Psalms 9 and 10 were originally a single psalm, in an acrostic form (cf. JB, NEB), but it is clear that in their present form they have been edited to form two distinct psalms: see P. C. Craigie, *Psalms 1—50* (Word Biblical Commentary 19; Waco, Texas: Word Books, 1983), pp. 116—17.

2 On these psalms, see C. Westermann, *Praise and Lament in the Psalms* (Edinburgh: T. & T. Clark, 1981), Parts 4 and 7; W. Brueggemann, 'Psalms and the Life of Faith: A Suggested Typology of Function', *Journal for the Study of the Old Testament* 17 (1980), pp. 3—32; W. Brueggemann, *The Message of the Psalms: A Theological Commentary* (Augsburg Old Testament Studies; Minneapolis: Augsburg, 1984), chapter 3; J. F. Craghan, *The Psalms: Prayers for the Ups, Downs and In-Betweens of Life* (Wilmington, Delaware: Michael Glazier, 1985), chapter 6.

3 e.g. A. Weiser, *The Psalms: A Commentary* (Old Testament Library; London: SCM Press, 1962), p. 93.

4 cf. W. Brueggemann, 'Theodicy in a Social Dimension', *Journal for the Study of the Old Testament* 33 (1985), pp. 3—25.

5 J. W. de Gruchy, *Cry Justice: Prayers, Meditations and Readings from South Africa* (London: Collins, 1986), p. 122.

6 H. Gollwitzer, K. Kuhn, R. Schneider, ed., *Dying We Live: The Final Messages and Records of Some Germans Who Defied Hitler* (London: Collins, ²1958), p. 86.

7 ibid., pp. 87—8.

8 This translation is from Craigie, *Psalms*, p. 121.

9 Westermann, *Praise*, p. 260. For other examples of this sequence in the Old Testament, see W. Brueggemann, 'From Hurt to Joy, From Death to Life', *Interpretation* 28 (1974), pp. 3—19.

10 Brueggemann, *Message*, p. 64.

11 'Come, Freedom, Come', in T. Couzens and E. Patel, ed., *The Return of the Amasi Bird: Black South African Poetry 1891—1981* (Johannesburg: Ravan Press, 1982), p. 157. The poem was first published in July 1950.

12 Z. Kameeta, *Why, O Lord? Psalms and Sermons from Namibia* (Risk Books; Geneva: WCC, 1986), pp. 1—3.

13 H. Camara, *The Desert is Fertile* (London: Sheed & Ward, 1974), pp. 17—19.

14 J. H. Reumann, 'Psalm 22 at the Cross: Lament and Thanksgiving for Jesus Christ', *Interpretation* 28 (1974), pp. 39—58.

15 Brueggemann, *Message*, p. 12.

16 H. Lilje, *The Valley of the Shadow* (London: SCM Press, 1950), p. 78.

17 J. Goldingay, 'On dashing little ones against the rock', *Third Way* 5/11 (1982), p. 25.

18 D. Bonhoeffer, *Letters and Papers from Prison* (London: SCM Press, 1971), p. 279.

19 Brueggemann, *Message*, pp. 85—7.
20 Lilje, *Valley*, p. 103.
21 J. M. Washington, ed., *A Testament of Hope: The Essential Writings of Martin Luther King, Jr.* (San Francisco: Harper & Row, 1986), p. 219.
22 I follow W. Beyerlin, *We are like Dreamers: Studies in Psalm 126* (Edinburgh: T. & T. Clark, 1982), whose interpretation of the psalm hinges on this unusual understanding of v. 1b. His argument has not been universally accepted: cf. L. C. Allen, *Psalms 101—150* (Word Biblical Commentary 21; Waco, Texas: Word Books, 1983), pp. 169—75.
23 RSV, as adapted in Beyerlin, *We are like Dreamers*, p. 59.
24 Beyerlin, *We are like Dreamers*, pp. 33—44.
25 Quoted in Washington, ed., *Testament*, p. 217.
26 J. Moltmann, *Experiences of God* (London: SCM Press, 1980), p. 8.
27 A. A. Anderson, *The Book of Psalms*, vol. 2 (New Century Bible; London: Marshall, Morgan & Scott, 1972), p. 866; Weiser, *Psalms*, p. 762.
28 Weiser, *Psalms*, p. 763.
29 Washington, ed., *Testament*, p. 219.
30 Kameeta, *Why, O Lord?*, p. 45.

Chapter 5

1 In this chapter I treat the relevant gospel passages as giving reliable historical information about Jesus. I take this approach to be warranted by the Gospels themselves, whose first readers could not have avoided reading them as being about a past in some respects different from their present. Thus Matthew (writing, I take it, after AD 70) tells the story of the temple tax (Matt. 17.24—7) and the story of Jesus' demonstration in the temple (Matt. 21.12—13) as stories of Jesus' reaction to historical realities which no longer existed when Matthew wrote, after the destruction of the temple. (The Romans substituted a Roman tax for the Jewish temple tax, but Jesus' argument in Matt. 17.25—6 would make no sense at all with reference to this Roman tax.)
2 My translation. For the interpretation of this passage which I follow below, I have argued in detail in 'The Coin in the Fish's Mouth', in *Gospel Perspectives 6: The Miracles of Jesus*, ed. D. Wenham and C. Blomberg (Sheffield: JSOT Press, 1986), pp. 219—52. See also the important article by W. Horbury, 'The Temple tax', in *Jesus and the Politics of His Day*, ed. E. Bammel and C. F. D. Moule (Cambridge: Cambridge University Press, 1984), pp. 265—86.
3 cf. K. Wengst, *Pax Romana and the Peace of Jesus Christ* (London: SCM Press, 1987), pp. 26—37.
4 Babylonian Talmud, *Shabbat* 33b.
5 In this section, I summarize the detailed argument to be found in my

article, 'Jesus' Demonstration in the Temple', in *Law and Religion*, ed. B. Lindars (Cambridge: James Clarke, 1988).

6 On the coins, see H. St J. Hart, 'The Coin of "Render unto Caesar ..."' (A note on some aspects of Mark 12:13–17; Matt. 22:15–22; Luke 20:20–26)', in Bammel and Moule, ed., *Jesus*, pp. 241–48.

7 The term 'Zealot' has been widely used to describe the whole movement of Jewish resistance to Rome from the time of Judas the Galilean to the fall of Jerusalem in AD 70. Probably this broad use of the term is inaccurate (Josephus applies it only to a specific group of revolutionaries in Jerusalem from AD 66 to 70), but I follow it here for convenience. The whole movement did have some continuity and coherence.

8 For this paragraph, see F. F. Bruce, 'Render to Caesar', in Bammel and Moule, ed., *Jesus*, pp. 254–57; E. Schürer, *The History of the Jewish People in the Age of Jesus Christ (175 B.C.–A.D. 135)*, revised by G. Vermes, F. Millar and M. Black, vol. 2 (Edinburgh: (T. & T. Clark, 1979), pp. 603–4.

9 *Pace* Bruce, 'Render to Caesar', pp. 259–60.

10 I owe this point to J. D. M. Derrett, 'Luke's Perspective on Tribute to Caesar', in *Political Issues in Luke–Acts*, ed. R. J. Cassidy and P. J. Scharper (Maryknoll, New York: Orbis Books, 1983), p. 42. In the financial context of 1 Chronicles 26, verses 30 and 32 probably refer to two categories of taxation, whereas in 2 Chronicles 19.11 the two phrases refer to two types of legal case. In view of the obscurity of these Old Testament passages, Jesus' saying probably presupposes that the phrases were used in contemporary Jewish legal discussion.

11 e.g. J. S. Kennard, *Render to God: A Study of the Tribute Passage* (New York: Oxford University Press, 1950); Wengst, *Pax Romana*, pp. 58–61.

12 cf. Bruce, 'Render to Caesar', pp. 255–56.

13 For a sketch of the issues involved here, see R. M. Green, 'Ethics and Taxation: A Theoretical Framework', *Journal of Religious Ethics* 12 (1984), pp. 146–61.

Chapter 6

1 See J. M. Court, *Myth and History in the Book of Revelation* (London: SPCK, 1979), pp. 148–52. For the cult of Roma in the cities of Asia, see D. Magie, *Roman Rule in Asia Minor to the End of the Third Century after Christ* (Princeton: Princeton University Press, 1950), pp. 1613–14; S. R. F. Price, *Rituals and Power: The Roman Imperial Cult in Asia Minor* (Cambridge: Cambridge University Press, 1984), pp. 40–3, 252, 254.

2 R. H. Charles, *A Critical and Exegetical Commentary on the Revelation of St John*, vol. 2 (International Critical Commentary; Edinburgh: T. & T. Clark, 1920), p. 65.

3 A. Y. Collins, 'Revelation 18: Taunt-Song or Dirge?', in *L'Apocalyp-*

Notes

tique johannique et l'Apocalyptique dans le Nouveau Testament, ed. J. Lambrecht (Gembloux: J. Duculot/Leuven: University Press, 1980), p. 201.

4 Quoted in K. Wengst, *Pax Romana and the Peace of Jesus Christ* (London: SCM Press, 1987), p. 9.

5 cf. Court, *Myth*, pp. 139–42.

6 cf. A. Farrer, *The Revelation of St John the Divine* (Oxford: Clarendon Press, 1964), p. 189; details in Charles, *Revelation*, vol. 2, pp. 95–113; A. Vanhoye, 'L'utilisation d'Ezéchiel dans l'Apocalypse', *Biblica* 43 (1962), pp. 436–76.

7 cf. G. R. Beasley-Murray, *The Book of Revelation* (New Century Bible; London: Marshall, Morgan & Scott, 1974), p. 264: 'This city summed up in itself and surpassed the wickedness of the tyrant-powers of the past.'

8 Revelation 18.14, my translation.

9 Oration 26: 11–13, translation from P. Aelius Aristides, *The Complete Works*, tr. C. A. Behr, vol. 2 (Leiden: E. J. Brill, 1981), p. 75. See also the literature cited in Wengst, *Pax Romana*, p. 186, n. 183.

10 Most of the following details derive from W. Barclay, *The Revelation of John*, vol. 2 (Daily Study Bible; Edinburgh: Saint Andrew Press, 1960), pp. 200–11, where other illustrations will also be found.

11 The phrase is from Juvenal 10:81.

12 On the Roman corn dole, see M. I. Finley, *The Ancient Economy* (London: Hogarth Press, 1985), pp. 198–204.

13 G. B. Caird, *A Commentary on the Revelation of St John the Divine* (London: A. & C. Black, 1966), p. 227.

14 A. A. Boesak, *Comfort and Protest* (Edinburgh: Saint Andrew Press, 1987), pp. 121–2.

15 Caird, *Revelation*, p. 227.

16 cf. Wengst, *Pax Romana*, p. 26.

17 M. Rostovtzeff, *Rome* (New York: Oxford University Press, 1960), p. 264. Note that John includes the *nauclēroi*, the shipowners, among the merchants of verse 11, and so does not list them among the mariners of verse 17, where the list begins not with the owners, but with the captains of the ships.

18 cf. Aelius Aristides, Oration 26:11–13. Wengst's comments (*Pax Romana*, p. 130) on the Mediterranean Sea as a negative image in Revelation are worth pondering in this connection.

19 18.20 is certainly not, as some English versions (including the RSV: I have slightly altered the punctuation to make my point) make it, part of the lament by the mariners.

20 See especially C. J. Hemer, *The Letters to the Seven Churches of Asia in their Local Setting* (JSNT Supplement Series 11; Sheffield: JSOT Press, 1986).

21 Hemer, *Letters*, pp. 87–94, 117–23.

22 The fact that the verb *sphazō* 'to slay', is used of the Lamb in 5.6, 9, 12; 13.8, and of the Christian martyrs in 6.9, is no proof to the contrary, for John also uses it of general slaughter in war in 6.4.
23 Quoted in Wengst, *Pax Romana*, p. 10.
24 cf. Wengst, *Pax Romana*, pp. 11–19.
25 Wengst, *Pax Romana*, p. 129.
26 cf. B. Goudzwaard, *Idols of our Time* (Downers Grove, Illinois: Inter-Varsity Press, 1984), chapter 5: 'The Ideology of Material Prosperity'.

Chapter 7

1 E. Bloch, *The Principle of Hope* (Oxford: Basil Blackwell, 1986), p. 258.
2 For a brief survey of relevant New Testament words, see R. T. France, 'Liberation in the New Testament', *Evangelical Quarterly* 58 (1986), pp. 9–12.
3 S. Croatto, 'The Socio-historical and Hermeneutical Relevance of the Exodus', in *Exodus — A Lasting Paradigm*, ed. B. van Iersel and A. Weiler (Edinburgh: T. & T. Clark, 1987) = *Concilium* 189 (1/1987), pp. 126–9. For a contrary view, see J. Barr, 'The Bible as a Political Document', *Bulletin of the John Rylands University Library of Manchester* 62 (1980), pp. 286–7.
4 J. Moltmann, in E. Moltmann-Wendel and J. Moltmann, *Humanity in God* (London: SCM Press, 1983), p. 57; cf. Croatto, 'The Socio-historical and Hermeneutical Relevance', p. 127: 'the very name of the God of Israel is indissolubly bound up with the Exodus experience of oppression-liberation'.
5 cf. Isaiah 32.18; Jeremiah 30.10; Ezekiel 34.25–9; Zephaniah 3.13.
6 See, generally, H. W. Wolff, *Anthropology of the Old Testament* (London: SCM Press, 1974), pp. 199–205; C. J. H. Wright, *Living as the People of God: The Relevance of Old Testament Ethics* (Leicester: Inter-Varsity Press, 1983), pp. 178–82.
7 So C. J. H. Wright, 'What Happened Every Seven Years in Israel? Part 2', *Evangelical Quarterly* 56 (1984), pp. 193–201; but against this view, see, e.g., A. Phillips, 'The Laws of Slavery: Exodus 21.2–11', *Journal for the Study of the Old Testament* 30 (1984), pp. 51–66.
8 cf. Wolff, *Anthropology*, p. 202.
9 My translation.
10 cf. already in the Old Testament, 1 Kings 12.7.
11 Quoted in A. Passerin d'Entrèves, *The Notion of the State* (Oxford: Clarendon Press, 1967), pp. 204–5.
12 For the notion of multidimensional liberation, see J. Moltmann, *The Crucified God* (London: SCM Press, 1973), pp. 329–35.
13 For a brief account of the Church's later attitudes to slavery, see R. N. Longenecker, *New Testament Social Ethics for Today* (Grand

Rapids: Eerdmans, 1984), pp. 60—6.
14 On such distinctions, see A. O. Dyson, 'Freedom in Christ and Contemporary Concepts of Freedom', *Studia Theologica* 39 (1985), pp. 55—72.
15 For this kind of freedom in Paul, see B. Gerhardsson, *The Ethos of the Bible* (London: Darton, Longman & Todd, 1982), pp. 76—8.
16 On inner and outer freedom in the spirituals, see J. H. Cone, *The Spirituals and the Blues* (New York: Seabury Press, 1972), chapter 3; *idem, God of the Oppressed* (London: SPCK, 1977), chapter 7; *idem, Speaking the Truth: Ecumenism, Liberation, and Black Theology* (Grand Rapids: Eerdmans, 1986), pp. 31—4.
17 In this respect, the Old Testament paradigm of liberation through the Exodus, which ended in the subjugation and elimination of the Canaanites, is transcended in the New Testament understanding of liberation.

Chapter 8

1 Luther quoted in C. A. Moore, ed., *Studies in the Book of Esther* (New York: Ktav, 1982), p. 370.
2 B. W. Anderson, 'The Place of the Book of Esther in the Christian Bible', in Moore, ed., *Studies*, p. 130.
3 The probable external confirmation of the historicity of Mordecai himself seems to suggest this: see C. A. Moore, 'Archaeology and the Book of Esther', in Moore, ed., *Studies*, pp. 380—1.
4 cf. D. J. A. Clines, *The Esther Scroll: The Story of the Story* (JSOT Supplement Series 30; Sheffield: JSOT Press, 1984), pp. 10—11, 31—3.
5 C. A. Moore, *Esther* (Anchor Bible 7B; Garden City, New York: Doubleday, 1971), p. 34.
6 For the typical anti-Semitism of 3.8, cf. the expansions in Josephus and the Targums, quoted in L. B. Paton, *A Critical and Exegetical Commentary on the Book of Esther* (Edinburgh: T. & T. Clark, 1908), pp. 203—4; also S. M. Lehrman, *A Guide to Hannukah and Purim* (London: Jewish Chronicle Publications, 1958), chapter 6.
7 N. H. Baynes, ed., *The Speeches of Adolf Hitler April 1922—August 1939*, vol. 1 (London: Oxford University Press, 1942), pp. 740—1.
8 B. S. Childs, *Introduction to the Old Testament as Scripture* (London: SCM Press, 1979), p. 605; cf. Moore, *Esther*, pp. 35—6.
9 A. D. Cohen, '"Hu Ha-goral": The Religious Significance of Esther', in Moore, ed., *Studies*, p. 122.
10 For the comparison, cf. Moore's discussion of G. Gerleman's proposal in Moore, ed., *Studies*, pp. XLVI—XLVIII.
11 D. J. A. Clines, *Ezra, Nehemiah, Esther* (New Century Bible; London: Marshall, Morgan & Scott, 1984), p. 269.
12 Clines, *Ezra*, p. 271.

13 cf. the discussion in Clines, *Esther Scroll*, pp. 145–6, 152–7.
14 Clines, *Ezra*, p. 302.
15 cf. G. McConville, 'Diversity and Obscurity in Old Testament Books: A Hermeneutical Exercise Based on Some Later Old Testament Books', *Anvil* 3 (1986), pp. 45–6.
16 See J. Baldwin, *Esther* (Tyndale Old Testament Commentaries; Leicester: Inter-Varsity Press, 1984), pp. 100–2.
17 That power and reversal are major themes in Esther is stressed by S. B. Berg, *The Book of Esther: Motifs, Themes and Structure* (Ph.D. thesis; Vanderbilt University, 1977), chapter 4. (This thesis is now published by Scholars Press as SBL Dissertation Series 44.)
18 cf. A. Kirk, 'The Middle East Dilemma: A Personal Reflection', *Anvil* 3 (1986), pp. 231–58.
19 cf. K. Cragg, *This Year in Jerusalem: Israel in Experience* (London: Darton, Longman & Todd, 1982), chapters 2–3.
20 R. Gordis, *Megillat Esther* (New York: Rabbinical Assembly, 1974), p. 13. This chapter was written a few weeks before I heard Professor Emil Fackenheim's 1987 Sherman lectures, in the University of Manchester, on 'The Jew of Today and the Jewish Bible'. In one of these lectures (which are to be published) he sketched an interpretation of Esther in relation to Hitler and the Holocaust which closely resembles the interpretation offered in this chapter.

Chapter 9

1 Much of this chapter first appeared as 'The Genesis Flood and the Nuclear Holocaust: A Hermeneutical Reflection', *Churchman* 99 (1985), pp. 146–55.
2 I am treating Genesis 6–9 as a whole in its final canonical form. Source-critical questions, important as they are in other contexts, are not relevant to our present purpose.
3 G. von Rad, *Genesis* (Old Testament Library; London: SCM Press, 1972), pp. 120–1.
4 cf. C. Westermann, *Genesis 1–11: A Commentary* (London: SPCK, 1984), p. 477.
5 G. Lambert, 'Il n'y aura plus jamais déluge', *Nouvelle Revue Théologique* 87 (1955), pp. 601, 720.
6 B. W. Anderson, 'Creation and Ecology', in *Creation in the Old Testament*, ed. B. W. Anderson (Issues in Religion and Theology 6; Philadelphia: Fortress Press/London: SPCK, 1984), p. 158.
7 These links are important and not irrelevant to the nuclear threat, but would take us beyond the scope of the present chapter.
8 Westermann, *Genesis 1–11*, p. 477.
9 ibid.
10 cf. Westermann, *Genesis 1–11*, pp. 410–11.
11 It is probably not correct to interpret 'all flesh' (6.12, 13) as including the animals as also held guilty of 'violence': see Westermann, *Genesis 1–11*, p. 416.

12 Westermann, *Genesis 1−11*, p. 337.
13 D. Clines, 'Noah's Flood: I: The Theology of the Flood Narrative', *Faith and Thought* 100 (1972−73), pp. 139−40.
14 cf. K. Barth, *Church Dogmatics IV/1* (Edinburgh: T. & T. Clark, 1956), p. 27.
15 Westermann, *Genesis 1−11*, p. 424.
16 See my article, 'First Steps to a Theology of Nature', *Evangelical Quarterly* 58 (1986), pp. 229−44.
17 On this aspect of the Flood story, see also W. Granberg-Michaelson, *A Worldly Spirituality: The Call to Redeem Life on Earth* (San Francisco: Harper & Row, 1984), chapter 5.
18 J. Schell, *The Fate of the Earth* (London: Pan Books, 1982), p. 115.
19 See J. Schell, *The Abolition* (London: Pan Books, 1984), pp. 13−23.
20 In a sense it is true, as Peter Selby ('Apocalyptic − Christian and Nuclear', *Modern Churchman* 26 (1984), p. 9) says, that 'the covenant with Noah has been placed irrevocably into our hands', though it should not be forgotten that other threats to human survival, over which we would have no control, are still quite conceivable.
21 For further discussion of divine providence and human freedom in the nuclear situation, see my article, 'Theology after Hiroshima', *Scottish Journal of Theology* 38 (1986), pp. 583−601.
22 Once again, the humanist writer Jonathan Schell sees the implications of the nuclear threat more clearly than most Christians: 'The nuclear peril is usually seen in isolation from the threats to other forms of life and their ecosystems, but in fact it should be seen as the very centre of the ecological crisis' (*The Fate of the Earth*, p. 111).
23 D. Aukermann, *Darkening Valley: A Biblical Perspective on Nuclear War* (New York: Seabury Press, 1981), p. 127. On the topic of this paragraph, see the whole of Aukermann's excellent chapter 18. See also Granberg-Michaelson, *A Worldly Spirituality*, pp. 175−7.

Chapter 10

1 On Jesus' loving solidarity with people, see also my chapter (with Rowan Williams), 'Jesus − God with Us', in *Stepping Stones*, ed. C. Baxter (London: Hodder & Stoughton, 1987), pp. 21−41; and my article, 'Christology Today', forthcoming in *Scriptura* (1988).
2 In what follows I am indebted especially to M. Hengel, *Crucifixion* (London: SCM Press, 1977).

Index of Biblical References

Genesis
1.26, 28 15-16, 135, 140
4 11, 134, 137
6-9 ch. 9 *passim*
9.1-7 11
10.8-12 11
11 11, 93

Exodus
15.18 59
20.2 105
20.7 37
21.2-6 108
21.20-1, 26-7 108
22.17 34
22.21 39
23.6 42
23.9 39, 106
23.10-11 28
30.11-16 74

Leviticus
19 ch. 2 *passim*
19.9-10 12
19.18 107
19.33-34 106
20.11 34
25.39-55 39, 108
25.42 105, 112
27.1-7 32

Deuteronomy
10.17-19 43
14.28-9 28, 39
15.12-18 108-9
16.19 45

17.14-20 48
21.10-14 109
21.18-21 31
22.23-4 34
23.15-16 108-9
23.24-5 28
24.17-18 43, 106
26.7-8 59
32.35-6 67

Judges
8.22-23 48, 106
9 48

1 Samuel
8 46, 48-9, 77, 105-6, 128

2 Chronicles
19.6-7 43, 45

Esther
ch. 8 *passim*

Job
15.7-10 32
29.15 46
31.13-15 109
32.6-7 32

Psalms
8.4-8 15
9.19-20 67
10 53-60, 65
22 64-5
58.11 66
68.5 46

General Index

Printed in the United States
200013BV00002B/232-273/A